KT-164-381

YORKSHIRE
IN A CROMBIE

ONE MAN. ONE COAT. ONE COUNTY.

Craig Bradley

Relish Books

First published in 2005 by Relish Books, Leeds, UK.

READ MORE WITH RELISH
www.relishbooks.co.uk

ISBN 0-9547-844-3-X

Copyright: Craig Bradley 2005

www.craigbradley.com

The Right of Craig Bradley to be identified as the Author of the Work has been asserted by him in accordance with the Copyright, Designs and Patents Act 1988.

This book is sold subject to the condition that it shall not, by way of trade or otherwise, be lent, re-sold, hired out or otherwise circulated in any form of binding or cover other than that in which it is published and without a similar condition including this condition being imposed on the subsequent purchaser.

Cover Photograph: Jacqueline Beedle @ DoThat ☺ Design

Cover Design: Richard Hemingway @ DogEnd

A Catalogue for this book is available from the British Library.

RELISH NUMBER 4
All Rights Reserved

Produced by
Central Publishing Services
Royd Street Offices
Milnsbridge
Huddersfield
West Yorkshire
HD3 4QY
www.centralpublishing.co.uk

To a big coat and the little bloke who used to wear it.

THANK YOU

Gervase Phinn for his sound advice, encouragement and for telling me to clean it up. Ian McMillan, Oliver Mantell and Terry Fletcher for their kind words. Rob Endeacott at Relish Books for keeping cool. Richard Hemingway at DogEnd for his work on the cover. Jon Medcalf for debugging bugged-up computers. My Dad, Keith Bradley, for his stories. Margaret Beedle, who was often left holding the babies at short notice.

Above all, thanks to Jackie, for her patience, support, proof-reading, typing, suggestions, for knowing the difference between a chapatti and a chipolata, and for letting me get this thing out of my system. To Ben and Jack for the song and dance routines and for reminding me that I'm a Dad first and a writer second.

And finally to all the people of Yorkshire whose words I've used in this book.

KIRKLEES CULTURE AND LEISURE SERVICES	
ACC NO.	250591648
CLASS NO.	914.281
Order No.	CUL40391
Date	4.10.05
Price	6.99
Supplier	Relish books
Loc	RE

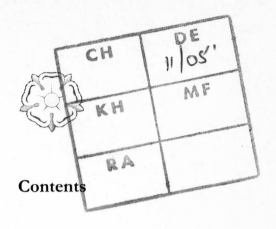

Contents

I don't care what the weatherman says
If the weatherman says it's raining
You'll never hear me complaining
                    Jeepers Creepers

I'm going where the sun keeps shining
Thru' the pouring rain
Going where the weather suits my clothes
                    Everybody's Talkin

Yorkshire In A Crombie

The Crombie

The word coat *has a tale to tell.*

It comes from the Old English word Cote *meaning shelter. I think we stole it from the French,* cotte, *who stole it from the German,* koth. *The Anglo-Saxons, the Dutch and the Icelanders also got involved, although what they actually did with the word is anyone's guess. They probably had a bit of a to-do, shook hands afterwards and got drunk. The French, just to be, well, French, turned Cote to Cotte and added the -age bit and, in doing so, turned a shelter into a cott-age. Cote has been about a bit. Everybody needs a home.*

As a name for a person, Yorkshire is full of coats. There's over fifty in the Huddersfield phone book alone. If you're a Mr or a Mrs Coat then you're in good company. As a name for a place, well, where do you start? There's Coates Cavern in Littondale and Muscoates near Pickering. There's Great Fencote and Little Fencote near Catterick. There's Dub Cote and Dub Cote Scar above Settle and Cote Pasture and Shaw Cote just outside Hawes. Then there's Oldcotes and Tullis Cotes in North Yorkshire and Carlcotes and Owlcotes in West Yorkshire. There's a Cote Lane in Bradford and a Cote Road in Halifax, a Cote Farm Lane in Shipley and a Cote Fields Avenue in Pudsey. There are loads more on the map but you can find those for yourself. They're here, there and everywhere. You can't move for coats in Yorkshire.

At school all my teachers looked like the cars they used to drive. Bully Boothroyd, dumpy and squat, drove a dumpy and squat Morris Eight. He taught music and played the piano like he was murdering someone. Mrs Kershaw was maths. She was small, smelt of old ladies and drove a Mini. Mr Lewis, the headmaster, was happy with mad hair and played the violin standing on his head. He had a Rover with a big shiny grill that always looked like it was smiling. Mr Briers was different, he didn't have a car. He didn't look like anything. But Ms Cowersley, she looked like something, oh yes indeed, a big something.

Ms Cowersley was a mystery. I never knew what her subject was, not that it mattered. Ms Cowersley was the first *Ms* I ever met. It made her different, exotic. She had long hair, short skirts and a sexy racing-green, Triumph Herald convertible. One look at Ms Cowersley and you grew up. She looked like she'd stepped straight out of a Martini advert.

As a school kid though, we weren't allowed to look like cars, we had to look like something else. But what? I went to school in the 70s. No rinky-dinky, super-duper camera phones for me, no iPods or portable DVD players. All I had was a Pop-a-Point pencil tucked in my pocket and a coat on my back. That was my lot. I'll shut up now because I sound like my Granddad. But the thing about not having a lot is that the little you do have becomes great. A pencil and a coat were all I needed.

Coats were important things. They were the first things people noticed about you. Mum would bang on and on about brushing your hair and polishing your shoes because that's what mums are for, bless em, that's what they do. But kids don't notice things like that, they couldn't give a monkey's. On that first day through those scary, black-iron, stuff-of-nightmares, school gates, it wasn't your well-groomed barnet or shiny size fives that singled you out, oh no, it was your coat that defined you, that said who you were and where you came from.

The first coat I remember was the Dufflecoat. It was navy blue and two sizes too big. Mum said I'd grow into it. I spent the first ten years of my life growing into things. The Duffle - I called it that because it sounded cool - flapped about a lot and made you look like the Grim Reaper when you put the hood up. I was glad to see the back of it. And what the hell are toggles when they're at home anyway?

Next was the Parka. Now this was more like it. It was khaki, the colour of wet cardboard. It had important pockets everywhere and a hood with fake fur that felt like a dead rabbit. The Parka wasn't just a coat though, it was a parachute. On blustery days you could pull it over your head and struggle, like a war hero, against the wind. If you were lucky you'd get blown clean off your feet.

The girls at school though never wanted to be war heroes. I couldn't understand them. I still can't. They were happy enough doing handstands against the wall and skipping. When they skipped they had little songs they used to sing:

Rain, rain, go away
Come back another day

Then they'd sing about a bloke called Doctor Foster who went to Gloucester - *in a shower of rain* – and one more where it was raining and pouring and the old man was snoring, whoever he was. I never sang those songs. Who likes songs full of rain? I had better stuff to sing about and I had a great coat to sing them in.

When you sang, the Parka came into its own. You could zip it up all the way, dig your hands in any pocket you like and let rip:

Ee by gum can your belly touch your bum?
Can your tits hang low, can you tie em in a bow?
Can you stand on your head till your knob turns red?

That was the first time I heard the phrase *Ee by gum*. I didn't know what it meant. I didn't know it was a piece of history, a juicy little bit of Yorkshireness. To me it was just part of the song and it rhymed with bum.

Gum, bum, gum, bum.

Perfect.

Everybody had Parkas at school, even the teachers. They wore sensible grown-up versions from the Army and Navy shop, the ones without the pockets and dead rabbit fur. Nobody said it but the teachers looked daft, like big kids. They had no idea. They didn't know the Parka rules, they didn't do the parachute, the singing or anything. Bless. They just didn't get it.

Then, around the time I was learning to shave, coats got put on the backburner, and I entered a strange and mysterious jacket phase. The Levi came first. It had to be a Levi, not a Wrangler, they were too cute and girly. Jackets for mummy's boys. A brand spanking new Levi came with its own ritual. You had to make it yours. It was like breaking in a horse. Fresh from the shop a Levi wouldn't do what it was told. They scratched and itched and rubbed the back of your neck. You had to wash it a million times just to get it to feel like a piece of clothing.

The Levi was a statement, it said something. It was supposed to say *Hey, look at me, I'm a serious rocker and I know my stuff.* What mine actually said was *Hey, look at me, I'm just a little pillock trying to look hard.*

Nuggets wore Levis as well. A nugget was someone who just liked the look but not the music. A cheat. To be a proper Levi man you had to know your Ozzy Ozbournes from your Angus Youngs, your Jimmy Pages from your Jimi Hendrixs. You had to know what Eddie van Halen had for his breakfast and what Phil Lynott had for his tea. Most importantly, you had to know the all words to *Smoke on the Water.* That one was a must.

Next up was the Leather Bomber jacket. Just to wear a jacket called a Bomber was the best thing in the world. You had to be careful with the Bomber though. Dad had a leather jacket, one he'd wear to go to the Royal Oak on Friday nights, and you had to make sure you didn't look like you were going with him. It wasn't a problem. You could turn the collar up, cover it in Deep Purple badges or get a jacket that was a touch too small. I liked the Bomber. I thought it made me look mean and menacing, like Brando in *The Wild One.* Looking back now I know who I really looked like. I looked like Dad.

After the Bomber came the Italian Combat jacket. Not a new one but a manky, second-hand one from a fat bloke down the market. It smelt of sweat and somewhere else. It had the Italian flag on the sleeve and the name *Carlo* sewn into the collar. I wonder if Carlo ever wore an old Crombie with my name stitched in it? The Combat had more pockets than the Parka and you could buy a pair of combat pants to match. A few mates went the whole hog and shelled out for jacket, pants, boots, hat and gloves. We looked like we were marching off to Monte Cassino. I bet that fatso down the market couldn't believe his luck.

When I started work I got a donkey jacket because that's what you did. The Donkey was black and woolly with shiny plastic bits on the elbows and shoulders. It had rubbish pockets and gave me a weeping red-rash. Just wearing it made you feel like one of those Irish navvies you see looking sheepish in black and white photographs. Like the Levi, the Donkey made a statement. It said *Look at me now, I'm all grown up*. I hated it. Who wanted to grow up? As a working jacket the Donkey had a problem; you couldn't work in it. It made you sweat before you got going, the rain soaked right through and it generally got in the way. I went back to the combat jacket, a jacket that could handle itself in the real world, and the Donkey went in the bin. *Hee-haw*, best place for it.

And then there's the Crombie.

On 19th March 2000 my Uncle Jim died. He was a dog-breeding, ballroom-dancing mechanic. During the war he worked in a tractor factory in Huddersfield making gearboxes for tanks. Jim was Dad's half-cousin, which made him a quarter relative somewhere down the line. He didn't look like one of us, he looked more like Danny Kaye. To me he always looked like he never got the joke, he had a face like a penny waiting to drop. Jim was small. So small in fact Dad used to say he looked like he'd fallen off a keyring. He had dog show trophies on his telly and photos of the winners all over the place: in the front room, kitchen, even in the loo. You'd go to his house, slope off for a pee and go nose to nose with a bulldog called Laughing Donald - *Crufts Best of Breed, 1972*. Jim was dead proud of Laughing Donald. He's more than just a dog, he'd say, waving an oily spanner at me, he's a little person. His best dogs had fancy show names like Little Duchess, Lovely Dawn, Lucky Devil. All their initials were LD after a mate of Jim's called Leonard Downs. Just think, if Leonard had been called Leonard Samuel Downs, it would have been a different story.

But anyway.

When Jim died his spanners went to my brother, the dancing

shoes to my sister, and where the dogs went is anyone's guess. I had my eye on his 1933 six-wheel Snubnose Morris. I could see myself tucked behind the wheel, crunching through the gears, honking my horn and winking at farmers' daughters. Instead, I got his crusty old Crombie. A coat that when wet was as heavy as a dead sheep. The farmers' daughters would have to wait.

Whenever one of his precious dogs had puppies Uncle Jim always used the Crombie as a makeshift birth-blanket. Over the years dozens of blind pink-nosed terriers lost themselves in its maze of pockets and sleeves. In the winter, when the weather turned, the coat doubled as an engine cover for the Snubnose - *The ice'll crack the gearbox clean in two as soon as look at it.* Given his eye for a well-turned-out ballroom dancer, I could see Uncle Jim Walter Raleighing the Crombie over puddles to impress the young ladies. All this gave the coat an interesting aroma, a pungent presence. So, with a pedigree of puppy pee, engine oil and old puddles, I tried the Crombie for size and looked at myself in the mirror. The mirror looked good.

It's hard to be yourself in another man's coat, to feel another man's fluff between your fingers. Mannerisms take on meaning. Old habits become new. Have I always walked like this? Fingered my ear-lobe? Sucked my teeth? When I put Uncle Jim's Crombie on I felt bigger, wiser, smellier. I felt like I could strip a gearbox at 30 yards and dance like Danny Kaye. The Crombie was kicking in. It was a suit of armour, a coat of arms. I was taking yesterday into tomorrow, taking something old into the new. I was full of history, full to the brim. I felt like if I stopped walking the Crombie would carry on without me, collar stiff and sleeves flapping into the future. Nothing could beat me now.

The Crombie has no straps or zips. No buckles or Velcro. No labels or logos. It's non-reversible. It hasn't got a hood and you can't fold it up and put it in your pocket. It is not a windcheater, a raincheater, or any kind of cheater. The Crombie doesn't cheat at all. It is a coat. *Cote.* Pure and simple, a coat for an honest man.

Or a shoplifter.

As a fashion statement the Crombie is a bit tongue-tied. It looks like the kind of coat a four-year-old would draw, a cartoon coat. It has two pockets, a collar and three big buttons down the front. The Crombie gets a reaction, people give you the once over. When you see them staring they look away really quickly and pretend to be doing something: fiddling with a mobile phone, waving to an invisible friend, picking their nose, anything is better than being caught making eyes at some crazy man in a big coat. Some people - the braver, drunker, more stupid ones - actually come up and ask you questions:

Are you wearing that for a bet?

Are you seeking asylum?

Are you some kind of weirdo-psycho, serial killer?

I always nod and say yes, especially to the last one.

The Crombie is a coat of contrasts. In the late 70s when my brother Mark started going out and learning how to drink, I used to sit on the bottom bunk-bed and pretend to be a DJ. Mark had LPs by bands like Madness, the Specials and Bad Manners. All these LPs had photos of the bands on the back looking hard in Crombies. Not smelly customised jobs like mine, but crisp, three-quarter length, velvet collared, pop-star versions. At the same time pipe-smoking Dales farmers also wore Crombies. They'd stand stroking their jaws, eyeing up bullocks and fondling rolled up tenners in king-size wads that could choke a donkey. I always suspected that these bull fanciers were secret Ska fans that played *One Step Beyond* on full volume and did the Madness Nutty Walk around Skipton Cattle Market when the doors were shut.

There are many Yorkshires. There's yours and there's mine. You know that beardy bloke who sells the *Big Issue* on the precinct? He's got his own Yorkshire. That nice smiley lady who lives two doors down, the one who knows your name but you don't know hers? She's got her own Yorkshire too. And what about that scary bloke on the train, the one who doesn't blink? Well he's *definitely* got his own Yorkshire and believe me, you don't want to go there. We've all got different ideas about the same place. There was Mum's Yorkshire: kids, Sunday dinners and daytrips to Scarborough. There's my sister's Yorkshire: kids, microwave dinners and hen-nights in Scarborough. And then there's my brother's Yorkshire: kids, no dinners and bollocks to Scarborough.

Mr Knobbs, my old woodwork teacher – he drove a battered old Ford Anglia so you can imagine what he looked like - had his own Yorkshire. Too right he did. He called it -*That God-forsaken hole between the Lakes and the Peaks.* But Knobbsy built a canoe that sank like a stone, so what does he know?

I met some bloke once who said that Yorkshire was to Britain what Bavaria was to Germany and Texas was to America. I was impressed. When I asked him what he meant, he said he hadn't a clue. He'd read it some time ago in some book going somewhere on some bus. It was some read.

There is a Yorkshire that talks in a telephone voice, wears *Hush Puppies* and minds its P's and Q's. A Yorkshire that has nicely pressed creases in its nicely pressed Sunday-best suit. A Yorkshire that never misses *Heartbeat* and laughs itself silly at *Last of the Summer Wine* repeats. A Yorkshire that drinks tea with its little pinky sticking out and lives in a cosy, cotton-wool world of village fetes, homemade jam, and having the vicar round on Sundays.

There is another version.

There is a Yorkshire that drinks, smokes and likes a flutter on the gee-gees. One that sweats, swears and messes around with loose women. A Yorkshire that sings too loudly at last orders and arm-wrestles bald, tattooed bouncers. There's a Yorkshire that looks you in the eye and gets on with it. A Yorkshire that knows a thing or two about a thing or two, about football and racing, about music and *Kes* and chicken bhunas, about getting stuck in and changing a gearbox on the hard-shoulder of the M62 when it's raining, because it's *always* raining. It knows all this, not through books or telly or surfing the web, but by the cuts and calluses on its hands, by the bags under its eyes and the beer in its belly. This Yorkshire has been around. It's been there and done it. It sings and it dances. This is my version. This is my Yorkshire.

The Olde Hatte is a pub slapbang in the town centre of Huddersfield. It's the kind of pub where you hear conversations like this:

Are you going to get drunk tonight?

No.

Why not?

I got drunk this afternoon.

One night, I asked Brian, the captain of the darts team, what he thought about Yorkshire. He paused and looked at me.

Yorkshire?

I nodded.

He paused again.

I've never been, he said.

Then he threw his last arrow and missed the board.

Bugger, he said.

What is Yorkshire? Is there such a thing as Yorkshireness? Do Yorkshire people have their own character? And how the hell did Brian manage to become captain of the darts team in *The Olde Hatte*? Like Brian though, I've also been missing the board. I've lived in Yorkshire all my life and I don't think I've ever been.

I had an idea.

I was going to put the Crombie on and have a look around this lump of land I call home. Why not? I'm going to roll up my sleeves and have a *real* look. Yorkshire can be a cold place so a big coat will come in handy. But the Crombie is about more than just keeping warm, any coat can do that. The Crombie is part of my past, it's a coat-cousin, the symbol of a Yorkshire I've only ever heard about. I never asked for the Crombie, it found me. It bided its time and singled me out. The Crombie isn't the kind of coat that wants to sit around all day, eating Hula Hoops and watching *Quincy* on cable. It wants to be out there, living it, that's what it's made for. The Crombie dared me to wear it and I did. So let's do it. Besides, seen one episode of *Quincy*, you've seen them all.

Like the Crombie, Yorkshire's a place of contrasts and contradictions, of ups and downs, ins and outs, blacks and whites. It's a beautifully ugly, massively small place. The population of Yorkshire is roughly the same as Scotland and the place is about as big as Jerusalem. So here I am wedged in this grey place, between the Highlands and the Holy Land and I need some answers.

Yorkshire needs a fresh coat of looking at and I reckon that Uncle Jim's Crombie is just the coat for the job.

Yorkshire Clockwise

It begins with a clock and a map.

In the kitchen, next to the clock, is a map of Yorkshire blu-tacked to the wall. Every time I do kitcheny things I look at it. I squeeze my teabags; I look at it. I burn my toast; I look at it. I ignore the washing up; I look at it. Then I look at the clock. Then back to the map again.

Clock. Map. Map. Clock.

Spoon. Jar. Jar. Spoon.

I started to put the two together in my head. I'd look at the map to find out the time then look at the clock and think of Yorkshire. When people asked me what time it was I'd say it was half past Doncaster. It was getting silly and I had to do something.

I did something.

I unblu-tacked the map and laid it on the kitchen table. Rotherham got covered in a blob of marmalade and Halifax got buttered, but hey that's life. Then I laid the clock over the map. I wanted to see what happened to the numbers, to see if they went anywhere. This is what I got:

One o'clock: *Ugglebarnby*
Two o'clock: *Silpho*
Three o'clock: *Sigglethorne*
Four o'clock: *Goole*
Five o'clock: *Blaxton*
Six o'clock: *Sheffield*
Seven o'clock: *Holme*
Eight o'clock: *Portsmouth*
Nine o'clock: *Wigglesworth*

Ten o'clock: *Hawes*
Eleven o'clock: *Richmond*
Twelve o'clock: *Potto*

Looking at those names it looks like a teamsheet for a Sunday League football side. Imagine the pre-match talk: Silpho, Sigglethorne get into em, Blaxton, keep it tight, make the ball do the work. Sheffield, Holme keep making those runs and Wigglesworth, if you see a chance have a go but whatever you do hit the bloody target. Potto, you're on the bench lad, now come on!

So all the players are in place but what about the hub, the linchpin? All these numbers can't just float about willynilly, they need to come from somewhere. I needed to find a centre, a middle to hang all these numbers on. I needed to find out just where the big hand meets the little hand on the face of my Yorkshire clock.

In Madrid there is a plaque on the pavement. It's a good-looking plaque that's no stranger to a duster and a spot of Mr Sheen. On its shiny surface it says that you are now standing in the dead-centre of Spain. The dead-centre. *I like that idea. I reckon if the Spanish can get it together and find the middle of an entire country then I can do the same for a county. And that was decided. I was off to find the pivot, the keystone of Yorkshire.*

What I really wanted was a ruin. A castle would do or a crumbling church. I wanted the hub of Yorkshire to have a real presence, a tangible meaning. I looked at the map, things started to spring into life. South of York the A64, A19, A63 and the A1 all come together to make a kind of lopsided square with a corner missing. The middle was hidden away in there somewhere. In there is where the Wharfe meets the Ouse and turns it the colour of a cheap chocolate milkshake. Now that would make a good centre-point, two rivers weaving and winding their way towards each other before finally merging together to become one. That's epic stuff and beats bolting a plaque to the pavement any day. Yeah that should be the middle, it really should.

But it isn't.

Slapbangwallop in the centre of Yorkshire is a field full of sheep. I know that because I've been. It's tucked between Appleton Roebuck and Acaster Malbis just below York. I leant on a rusty five-bar gate and watched the sheep being sheep. I could see two or three grain silos and heard a small plane that sounded like a flying lawnmower. There was no plaque. No fanfare or trumpets. There wasn't even a Post-it note stuck to a tree. But this was it. This was the fulcrum I was looking for. This is where the big hand meets the little hand. Here is where it starts.

One o'Clock: Ugglebarnby

Words are powerful things. The word *word* though, lets itself down. It's too hollow, too dry-as-dust, too woody. Say it quick and you're grunting, you've strained yourself and done your back in. Say it slowly and you have a ten-year-old Mondeo with a dodgy alternator farting on a foggy morning. The word *word* needs a bump start. How can something like *lackadaisical* be something called a word? It's alive and looks after itself. It's a symphony in A. Look at *piccalilli*. It's a typo, yes; an Italian clown, yes; Lucky Luciano's pet-name for his mistress, yes, yes, yes. A jar full of manky old vegetables nobody wanted, sliced, diced and stewed in vinegar?

No.

It is anything and everything except what it is. Just like Ugglebarnby.

Dickens would have been taken with Ugglebarnby. He'd be well into it. He'd like the shape it'd make of his mouth. I can see him now.

I've got this new book on the go.

Oh yeah. What's it called?

Ugglebarnby.

Ugglebarnby? Forget it Charlie. Stick to little match girls and orphans. That's what they want nowadays.

Ugglebarnby sounds prehistoric. Like something a caveman would have said when he stubbed his toe. It should be an ugly place. It really should. There should be an ugly bloke with ugly DIY prison tattoos leering by an ugly barn. There should be rusty hypodermic needles, old Tampax and last night's condoms clogging up the gutters. There should be no trees, no fields, no blue in the sky, no colour at all. There should be glue-sniffers going glass-eyed behind the gasworks. There should be *Baz is a Fat Bastard*, *Balls to Blair* and *Ryan Loves Kylie* spray-painted on ugly concrete walls. There should be. But there isn't.

Ugglebarnby doesn't do what it says on the tin. Not at all. It's the kind of place where your Grandma should live. In fact she probably does. She's probably sitting down right now watching *Antiques*

Roadshow and dunking digestives into her Typhoo.

Bless her cottons.

Ugglebarnby is one road. Walking through I pass a blue Lotus Esprit, a speedboat called Sheltie and a sprinkling of no-nonsense stone-built, detached houses. Next to the All Saints Church there is a bloke working on a house so big it looks like it's being built for a lottery winner. Money is in the air, bags of it. All you have to do is breathe in.

All Saints Church has something timeless about it. It could have been built 300 years ago or two weeks last Tuesday. I tried the door, it was locked. God wouldn't let me in. I stood there a minute, getting a sense of the place. Letting it rub off on me. I could imagine newlyweds, standing on this very spot, full of kisses, giddy with butterflies and confetti. I could see flustered parents holding hands and winking at each other over little pink babies. It was all there.

Except it wasn't.

There was something missing, something out of kilter. I sat on the step and looked across at fields so green they looked like they'd been airbrushed in. Then the penny dropped. Here I was in a graveyard and there wasn't one single grave. Not one. No headstones, no tell-tale mounds of earth. Nothing. All Saints looks like a church, it smells like a church but it doesn't *feel* like a church. It's not playing the game. It hasn't got a date-stone over the door, ugly wire mesh covers the stained glass windows and it's got a grave-less graveyard. Being a gravedigger in Ugglebarnby must be the cushiest job in the world.

Just outside Ugglebarnby is a war memorial in front of a chip shop. As you stand there, reading the names of the fallen, you hear the splash and sizzle of frying haddock, the please and thankyous and the ping of micro-waved pies. Men died for this. The memorial is well-tended and means a lot to someone. It comes complete with a chained-off mini garden and a poppy wreath. Tucked into the corner of the garden, looking like a dog that's just eaten your best shoes, was a sign saying B&B. 150 YARDS. Old soldiers may come and go but tourism marches on.

Ah well.

Driving south on the A169 I pass the giant sandcastle they call

RAF Fylingdales. God help us if they find the bucket and spade. I open the car window, put my elbow out and feel like Dad. I start singing *Wonderful World*. I'm belting it out. Why not? No-one's listening. The sky goes on forever and the heather smells like lavender. Everyone hates me; motorbikes, white-van men and petrol-heads in open top BMW Roadsters. They give it the big licks and overtake with attitude. I let them, who cares? I'm happy away, snailing along. I'm going to Pickering and Pickering is going nowhere.

I like Pickering. I always have done. I like the way it's not on the level, the way it slopes from the church at the top of Market Place to the bookies at the bottom. It's symbolic, rolling down from the saints to the sinners. You can pick your horse, bang a tenner on and then pray it romps home. I like the fact there's a pub called the Black Swan and one called the White Swan. It keeps the place balanced, stops it sinking into the muddy-murk of the North York Moors. In 1836 they had a bit of a do in the Black Swan to celebrate the opening of the Whitby to Pickering railway line. They had cannons, brass bands and all the rest of it. No soggy vol-au-vents or karaoke here. I would've loved to have been there, to have blown the froth off my flagon of ale, smack my lips and watch George Stephenson goosing all the barmaids. Sounds like a hoot.

I was putting off leaving. I didn't want to drive to Malton and pick up the A64 back to Leeds. I was happy sitting in the Black Swan, about as happy as happy gets. Pickering does that to you. It's a good place to step back and do nothing, a good place to breathe and be idle. The word I'm looking for is lackadaisical.

Two o'Clock: Silpho

Words that end with O do it for me. There's something about them.
Rambo was the first video I ever watched. I didn't understand a word
he was saying but I watched it anyway. When it finished I felt like I
could fight the world and win. I can watch Groucho, Harpo and
Chico till the cows come home, have a kip, make some butties and go
back to work again. Even Zeppo gets a thumbs up.

I want you to do something for me.

Close your eyes, lick your lips and purr the word *libido*. Go on. It
feels good.

Libido.

And again.

Libido.

See, suddenly you're a sex god.

When I was a kid I used to say *brillo* a lot. I just liked the sound of
it. It was my catchphrase.

Have you seen the *Beano*?

Yeah. It's brillo.

Do you like Mars Bars?

Yeah, they're brillo.

It was brillo this and brillo that.

What a weirdo.

I soon gave it a wide berth when I found out it was wire-wool
Mum used to clean the pans. Then there's Ego, Casino, Rodeo,
Ringo, Jingo, Limo, Lothario, Aero, Cluedo, Wacko Jacko and Zero.
You can't say em unless you sing em. And forget those sugar-coated
Italian beauties: Vino, Cappuccino, Bellisimo, Bambino, Robert De
Niro and Al Pacino. As for Sergeant Bilko? He's a hero, from his
pate to his pinkies. So, when I looked at the map and saw Silpho at
two on the Yorkshire clock. That was it.

Bingo.

We drove to Silpho from Scarborough. Dad came along to tut
and shake his head a lot when his useless son approached a road end
in the wrong gear. We were staying in a flat on Eastborough Road

above a shop called Chocolate Heaven.

Bloody ell, Dad said, can't get any higher than this.

How'd yer mean?

We're higher than heaven.

The flat had great views of the south beach, the castle and King Arthur's Tattoo Parlour. The sun terrace though was a no-no. That was serious seagull country. Those big-boys would nick your chips, shit on you and fly away laughing their little seagull heads off. We were easy pickings. They could spot a landlubber a mile away.

When in doubt turn left.

Dad says things like that. He also says things like:

When you go up to Scotland keep the sea on yer right, when yer coming home keep it on yer left.

We're not goin to Scotland, I said.

Where we goin?

Silpho.

Silpho?

Silpho.

Dad sniffs.

What for?

I shrug.

I like the sound of it, I say, besides I want to write about it.

Dad sniffs again. Loudly.

Aye well writing's one thing, he says, but who wants to bloody read it?

I had no answer.

We drove through Silpho on a zingyfresh spring morning and didn't see a soul. There was evidence of life going on - washing pegged on lines, deadpan cats on Freelanders, curtains in windows, that type of thing - but no actual human life. The street was empty, the duck pond was duckless, and the Methodist Chapel had been converted into a private house. Ey up, I thought, even God has left town.

Silpho has a village notice board - *Sponsored Horse Ride. Bring your horse and enjoy a day out in beautiful countryside.* Bugger, I thought, I've left my horse at home. Next to the notice board is a phone-box. A big red time machine type job. 01723-882228. Make that call. Go on. Liven the place up a little. Fifty quid says no one picks up.

Silpho is perched at the edge of Broxa Forest, next to a place called Whisperdales. Whisperdales is a good place to go and shout your head off. The sheep don't mind. Broxa Forest is peppered with tumuli. I didn't know what a tumuli was until I looked it up. It sounds like something you'd catch drinking dirty water. It isn't. It's an ancient burial mound. I thought it would be a wheeze to try and find one. Dad sniffed again.

Just what you want to do on a lovely sunny morning innit, he said, root for rotten bloody graves.

We rooted.

And rooted.

And rooted.

I wanted something out of Indiana Jones. Something that made the hair on the back of your neck crackle with static, a direct line to the past. A big, fat, juicy slice of physical history. I was thinking big. As big as Tutankhamen, The Tolland Man and The Holy Grail all rolled into one. I wanted something to smack me in the belly and make me feel *connected*.

What I got was a forest floor. Nothing else. Leaf-mulch, grass and loads of it. All that rooting though, made me realize one thing. I'd be crap on *Time Team*.

Craig Bradley

Three o'Clock: Sigglesthorne

The first thing I heard was the donkey laughing. Happy as Larry. I parked the car, got out and there he was, in a field opposite St Lawrence's Church in Sigglesthorne. There was a funeral going on in the church graveyard and a laughing donkey didn't fit the bill. Not at all. Somebody should have a word.

Sigglesthorne is half a dozen miles up the road from Beverley and St Lawrence's graveyard is about as good looking as graveyards get. It's not the kind of graveyard you'd see in a horror film. No gargoyles coming over all devilish and demonic in the shadows. No Freddy Kruger-ish goings on to worry about, just happy flowers and dead people sleeping off life's hangover. There was a freshly dug grave all ready and dressed up with grass mats. It looked kind of welcoming. The gravedigger had done a good job. He was sitting in his Escort thumbing his way through the sport pages of the *Daily Mirror*. Every now and again he'd look at me and flick fag ash out of the window. The mourners filed into church. Sober-suited, black-tied and funeral-faced. It was clear that whoever it was who'd left us was already being missed. It was all a bit unreal, a bit too English, whatever that means: picturesque village church, well kept graveyard, the air of quiet dignity? Think yourself lucky I'm not Bill Bryson or you'd be reading about this for a hundred pages. I felt like an extra in a 50s Ealing comedy. We even had a bumbling vicar who entered stage left and half-stumbled, half-staggered across the graveyard. He had a beard, grey hair and looked a sermon short of a service. I just hope he got the name right.

St Lawrence's was built in 1676, about ten years after Newton got hit on the bonce by a gravity bound Granny Smith's. A quick shufty at the noticeboard told me that it costs £9 to be baptised, £139 to be buried and £162 for a marriage service. Being born is £130 cheaper than dying, sounds like a good reason to stay alive, and being married costs more than being buried. Not to mention less spade work. I suppose it's all down to supply and demand. The more people want to get married the more the price goes up. If you got baptised,

20

married and buried at St Lawrence's you'd be £310 down on the deal. Not that you'd care. You'd be pushing up the daisies and the gravedigger would still be on the sporting pages.

In contrast to the timeless scene being played out at St Lawrence's was the building site on East Lane. Walking from the soft, sweet silence of the church and hearing the soft, sweet song of the pneumatic drill was like walking through a sci-fi time-gate. One that zapped me from the 18th century slapbang into the middle of the 21st. Dumpers were dumping, Caterpillars were caterpillaring and JCBs were JCB-ing. Everybody from the site foreman, the chippies, sparkies and brickies right down to the hod-donkeys and barrow-monkeys were wearing yellow hardhats and steel toe-capped rigger boots. The place was buzzing with graft. *Dangerous Area* signs were nailed to the perimeter fence and flags were flapping over the site office. What is it with modern building sites and flags? Maybe developers think that flags add a dramatic sense of occasion, a touch of affordable palatial splendour?

They don't.

They just make the place look like a circus. Building sites are ugly, dangerous, noisy, sweaty, blister-making, backbreaking places. Flags are for dead kings and sandcastles. Let's keep it that way.

Sigglesthorne has no shop, Post Office or pub. What it does have is a primary school. You can't buy a loaf of bread, a stamp or a pint in Sigglesthorne but you can learn to fingerpaint and make chocolate cornflake buns, so it's not all bad. There are two kinds of primary school. Old, dark ones built from stone and modern, shiny ones built from brick. My primary school was big, scary and Victorian. And that was just the teachers.

When I got back to the car the donkey was still there. As I started the engine I heard him laugh again. I drove out of Sigglesthorne and looked back at him. I was wrong, he wasn't laughing. He was just smiling, loudly.

Four o'Clock: Goole

Goole was famous at school. Everyone talked about it. It had top billing in a gag that knocked about the playground.

Y'know Yorkie Bars are called Yorkies because they're made in York?

No.

It's a good job they weren't made in Goole innit?

Hardly a classic I know but it was better than getting kicked black and blue playing British Bulldogs with Mental Macko and Hard Bob Briggs.

The thing is though, Goole meant more to me than I let on. I knew things about Goole, proper, important, grown-up things. Things no-one else knew I knew.

I knew it had a dockyard.

I knew what it looked like.

I knew where it was.

I'd point it out in Mr Daniels' geography lesson.

It's there sir, I'd say, smugging it up, that's where Goole is.

And I'd be bang on the money, every time. When it came to Goole I was your man, the head honcho. I just *knew* stuff, a lot of stuff. And I knew because Mum told me.

Mum lived in Goole during the war. Not the best idea in the world considering Hitler did his best to flatten it. Not personally obviously. Like any dictator worth his salt he was miles away from the messy stuff. He left that to the Luftwaffe. When those Teutonic terror-boys got cheesed off blitzing Hull they'd let a few 40-pounders loose on Goole docks. Just for the hell of it. I suppose it kept the job interesting. Maybe the apprentice bomber pilots cut their teeth on Goole. Maybe German pilots who'd sat on their specs and had *ein* too many in the *bierkeller* aimed for Hull but hit Goole instead. Or maybe those guys just couldn't hit a cow's arse with a banjo.

Whatever.

When those bombs fell on Goole, Mum and her brother Jack were tucked up in Jackson Street, nice and snug, in a cupboard under the stairs. Mum's mother was sat in her rocking chair singing. She sang songs she knew and some she didn't. Words didn't matter, the singing was the thing. The singing and the noise it made. As long as the bombs dropped she sang. I don't know where she found the breath. She sang for her children and she sang for herself, as loud as she could. Louder than Messerschmitts, louder than doodlebugs, louder than war.

Because her Dad, Bill, was in the police, Mum moved about a bit. She was born in Bradford, moved to Goole before going on to Doncaster, Halifax and Barnsley. She should be the one writing this book. I'd have lent her the Crombie. She'd have looked good in it. In the early 50s Mum lived in the police house in Royston, near Barnsley. The house was part of the police station and there were some cells in the cellar. On the weekends Mum used to take breakfast down to the prisoners. We're not talking murderers, rapists or big-time baddies here, just hung-over scallys snoring off the night before. If they ever invent a time machine I have a plan. I'm going to have a skinful in 1950s Royston and get thrown in the clink by my Granddad. Then I'm going to sit on my bunk and watch my fifteen-year-old mother tiptoe down the cellar-steps with a full mash. As I take the plate off her, I'll give her a wink, nothing fancy, just a little one, sly enough to give me an air of mystery. I'll be happy and Mum'll skip back up the steps thinking I'm a lovable rogue. Then I'll lick the plate clean and zip back to the future with a full belly and a big smile. Job's a goodun. Mum knew her way round a kitchen. It would have been a breakfast worth getting banged up for.

Mum's mother's name was Elsie Watson but everyone called her Nanan. Not Gran, Nan or Nanny; other people had one of those, but we had Nanan. Nothing more, nothing less. Saying the word now it sounds like somewhere rich people go on their holidays – *You've not been to Nanan? You simply must, it's a dream and the sunsets are to die for -* but back then it meant Mum's Mum and that was that. When her husband died in Royston in 1952, Nanan came to live in Halifax. She got a flat over a chip shop and a job at the sweet factory. It was whilst living there that Mum met Dad and one thing led to another which kind of led to me.

Nanan's flat was an Aladdin's cave. She had a big brandy balloon on the windowsill. I don't know why, it never saw any brandy. Instead it had a pot mouse sat in the bottom of it looking up at a pot cat that was trying to climb in over the top. I never got that. What the hell was a mouse doing in a brandy glass? Are they fond of the odd tipple? Maybe rats like a drop or two of the hard stuff, maybe that's where the term rat-arsed comes from. Try calling someone mouse-arsed and see how far you get. Then there was the cut-glass salad bowl. This came complete with cut-glass fork and spoon. Somehow, when Nanan died in 1987, this fell into my hands. Now all I need is a cut-glass tomato and I'm away. Nanan also had a hipflask that wasn't so much a hipflask as a cough medicine bottle in disguise. Nanan was always doing that, making things into things. She'd make Christmas decorations out of egg boxes and woolly hats out of old jumpers. You had to keep moving round at hers or she'd turn you into a tablecloth. The one thing I most remember though is the silver cigarette holder. Nanan was a big-time smoker, everybody in the world smoked then. She stopped when she was seventy-five and went downhill fast until the doctor told her to start again – *Can I get them on prescription?* she asked. The cigarette holder was a little gem. It felt slim and cool in your hand. Just holding it made you feel like James Bond. If you pressed a little button on the top it sprung open like a trap. All the cigs would be lined up inside, neat and tidy, like little soldiers ready for action. It was never empty even though Nanan *always* had a fag on the go. That was part of its magic. There was an inscription engraved on the inside:

Smoke like Helen B Merry.

There it was in fancy swirly writing.

Smoke like Helen B Merry.

Classic.

I kept saying it and saying it. It was the best joke I'd ever seen. It put the one about Yorkies coming from Goole in the shade. Nanan had to spell it out to some of the others but not me. I had it sussed from the off. Nanan, Helen B Merry and me shared something. Something unsaid. We had a bond, a connection. We were all singing from the same hymnsheet, and Nanan, being true to form, was singing the loudest.

I remember the snow.

It wasn't making a social call. It meant business. Forget the fluffy cotton-wool, amateur kind, this was the ugly, gutter-hugging, sod-yer-an-spit-in-yer-eye professional stuff. The sky was full and settled in for the day. My brother Mark, my brother-in-law Glenn, cousin Steve and me were on pall-bearing duty. They looked focused, in control, like men with a mission. I was just concentrating on staying on my feet.

What if I slip?

You won't.

I know but what if I do?

We'll be reight, Mark said.

I wasn't convinced.

I took the cough medicine-cum-hipflask out of my pocket and had a nip. Twelve-year-old Glenlivet. The good stuff Mum saved for special occasions. When it hit the back of my throat it made my face go funny.

Steve gave me the once over.

That won't help your footing, he said.

My footing had nothing to do with it.

I had another nip. I could taste the smoke, the wood, the wet muck.

A drop of Dutch, I said.

We picked the coffin up.

We had a problem.

Mark, Glenn and me are all about six foot, give or take, Steve wouldn't be over five foot six if he was wearing pink stilettos with five inch heels.

I checked.

He wasn't.

I was sharing the front end with him. The coffin went down sharpish at one corner.

Right, Steve said to me, you'll have to bend down a bit.

I bent down a bit.

A bit more.

A bit more.

Glenn was grunting behind me. I felt like the front end of a pantomime horse. Steve still wasn't happy.

Just a touch more, he said, that's it, that's it.

And we were off. I went into the church, carrying Mum's coffin, walking like Groucho Marx.

This is the part of the film where I get the cigarette holder out, smile at *Helen B Merry* and spark one up. Then I put it in my pocket, wink at the stars and walk away, blowing smoke over the closing credits. The only sound you hear is Nanan, shown in grainy flashback, singing under those stairs in Goole. Nothing else, just that one voice, as loud now as it was then, ringing out across the years, clear as day.

Five o'Clock: Blaxton

It was one of those bracing mintyblue mornings. The air was toothpaste and everything was crisp and sharp. The world was laid out before me like a freshly pressed shirt. Your breath came out in clouds and made you look like a chain-smoking 40s movie star. For one mad, Walter Mitty minute I was Bogart, casually packing his piece and making his way across town to some crazy dame's gin joint on the Lower Eastside. When the bubble burst I realized I don't smoke, I haven't got a gun and I was going to Blaxton.

Oh, and I'm not Bogart neither.

Turn off the M62 onto the M18 and you enter another world. The landscape is so flat it plays tricks on you. It's like being trapped in a life-size optical illusion. Everything is even and unbroken. There's nothing to lock into, to aim at. Your sense of perspective goes out the window. There's the odd farm sprawled about but it's hard to tell if they are far away or just really, really small. You start to feel like the car is standing still and the outside is moving. The road itself looks longer than it is. Like the one on the cover of The Eagles *Greatest Hits*. There's bound to be a mad-eyed bloke with a nervous tic and spit in his beard that's been driving non-stop on the M18 since 1986. I'm not knocking it, I like space. There should be more of it. It's just a bit unnerving for someone who comes from a place where you have to walk up a dozen hills just to buy a pint of milk and some Hobnobs. I'm always suspicious when I see postmen on bikes. You don't get that in Halifax, Huddersfield or Bradford, the price of stamps would go through the roof.

On the way into Blaxton I pass signs for the Moorhouse and Lindholme prisons. That's more like it. The chance of seeing Fletch and Godber tear-arsing their way to freedom across a field always gives a place a certain buzz. I looked but didn't see anything. Ah well, it is cold. Best stay indoors. Either that or they're tunnelling out right now. I whistled the theme tune from *The Great Escape* as I drove past. You've got to do your bit.

Blaxton is a roundabout, a scatter of houses and a 30s scout hut they call a village hall. There's a 19ᵗʰ century Wesleyan Chapel but it's got broken windows and big prisoner-proof padlocks on the door so it doesn't really count. By the roundabout was a pub called the Blue Bell. Fastened to the front of the pub was a big OPEN ALL DAY banner. Things were looking up. I tried the door. It was locked. I tried again. Still locked. I would have broken in but I didn't have a crowbar on me. Typical. There's never a thief around when you want one.

On the roundabout two blokes were fixing a bollard. No they weren't. One bloke was fixing it and his mate was doing his best to look interested. Either that or he was trying to work out why the Blue Bell was shut. I walked round Blaxton roundabout clockwise then I walked round anticlockwise. Then, for the hell of it, I walked around clockwise again. Then I got dizzy and called it a day. I was all Blaxtoned out. I went back to the car, sat for a while and watched the windows steam up. I looked at my map and started the car. At times like this there is only one thing you can do.

Go to Doncaster.

London has The Smoke, Edinburgh has Auld Reekie and Doncaster has Donny, more an abbreviation than a nickname but you've got to start somewhere. When I was a kid in the 70s Donny meant a clean-living God-botherer popstar with loads of brothers and even more teeth. Now Donny means something else. It's part of a Yorkshire trend. It's up there with Ponty Carlo and Cas Vegas. Donny is cool. It's arrived. But then again it never really went anywhere.

The world's a lonely place when you're dying for a pee and can't find a toilet, a really lonely place. You ask people for the nearest loo and they um and ah and give you long-winded directions that you can't follow because things are getting serious and you can't concentrate. Then you see the signs. But what do signs know? They're only signs. They have no sense of urgency. Pensioners are your best bet. Take it from me. They tend to know these things, the nearest toilets and bus timetables. I walked into the Frenchgates Shopping Centre and asked the first old lady I saw.

Toilets? she said.

I nodded.

For you love?

I nearly said no, for that bloody bloke over there, but I didn't. I thought another nod might be a better idea.

Well there's some across the way there, but there's allus young uns in there messing abart an stuff. You want BHS love, they're nice ones they are. Clean. Down there second on your left.

The good news is she was right. The bad news is they were closed. First the Blue Bell, now this. It's enough to make you paranoid. I could picture burly KGB types whispering into their collars - *There's Bradley, keep him out of the pubs and don't let him pee. That'll sort him.* In the end I snuck into a swanky café called Coffee Club, did what I had to do and sloped out without putting a down-payment on a cappuccino.

Close call.

It was only four when the streetlights buzzed a bit and flickered on. The sky looked like the beginning of a Hammer Horror film as I mooched around Donny under a Peter Cushing moon. The weather went from bracing to somewhere the other side of freezing. Everybody took on a bit of a rosy-glow. I looked at people milling about, at those standing at bus stops and cash-point queues. The cold didn't bother them. Not a bit. Most of them had a resigned sort of look. It was a look I saw in the men and women, the young and old. They looked hard. Not hard in a oi-what-you-looking-at sense but in a whatever-life-throws-at-me-I'll-pick-it-up-and-throw-it-back kind of way. Two old ladies, who must have been tuned into all this, stood behind me talking.

Your husband though, said one, he's a proper fighter int he?

He bloody is that, said the other, y'know he dint know he'd had a stroke till t'doctor told him.

See what I mean.

Six o'Clock: Sheffield

In the 80s my sister Kay bought an old railway carriage. As you do. It was a pile of rust and cobwebs but she had a vision. Big sisters are like that. Kay got busy. She gave it a lick of paint, fitted a hotplate and there you go, she had a burger-bar. It was parked in a lay-by off Manchester Road, coming out of Sheffield, and the door was flung open for business. I'd go and eat burger after burger till I could burger no more. Then I'd swill it all down with free polystyrene tea and belch. I knew then that the world really was wonderful.

It didn't last.

On New Year's Day 1988 I woke up with a head full of never-again and a bellyful of Auld Lang Syne. I clicked the radio on and somebody with a serious voice told me that Rick Allen, Def Leppard's drummer, had lost his arm in a car crash. Leppard were a bunch of Sheffield plank-spankers who sold a gazillion albums in the States. Leppard did all the rock star stuff: tight pants, dodgy mullets, fast cars, but they didn't speak like rock stars, they spoke like miners, like out of work welders, like me. They were Yorkshire to the bone and America went nuts for them. Leppard had a theory:

Big hair + Big guitars = Big music

and I was well into it, but I was more than just a fan. I was proud of them and you know what, I still am.

Rick had been driving his Corvette Stingray along Manchester Road near Kay's burger-bar. He'd lost control on a zigzaggy bend and ploughed straight into a dry stone wall. Rick was thrown out of the car but his arm stayed put. Suddenly the big world outside was rubbing its nose up against the window of my own little one. I clicked the radio off, popped a paracetamol and decided to go back to sleep. I thought that when I woke up, the headache will have gone, Rick's arm will be back where it should be and everything will be alright. I knew it was a long shot but at that moment a long shot was all I had.

Sheffield is Rome. It's built on seven hills, it has a river and it has two football teams, admittedly one is called after the most boring day of the week but let's not go into that. As well as Rome, Sheffield is Prague, Berlin and Budapest. Walking round Sheffield is like flicking through the *Lonely Planet Guide to Europe.* It looks, feels and smells like a grimy old European city. I know Sheffield *is* a grimy old European city but you know what I mean. It has that up-for-anything, been-there-done-that, lived-in look. It's the trams that do it, gliding about being all smug and efficient. Up on Church Street, by the Cathedral, they create this snappy mix of old and new that gives the city a real Eurobuzz. Sheffield is a great place to wear better shirts, drink better beer and practice being European. I reckon the Prime Minister and his cronies should move up here. Give the whole EU thing a proper stab.

I sat down on the precinct to watch the world go by. An old lady wrestling with half a dozen plastic bags came and sat next to me. She moved some of her bags around and got comfy.

Y'know, she said, that you can taste what a pig's been eating before it's killed, did you know that love?

I shook my head.

Oh yes, she said, my uncle kept one and fed it nothing but custard, big buckets of the stuff, well, when he killed it we had custard flavoured bacon for weeks.

I looked around for some men in white coats. I didn't see any.

The bag lady laughed and pointed at me.

I always keep brown paper bags, old light bulbs and dead batteries, she said.

She was speaking like there was a war on.

She struggled to her feet and tapped her nose.

Because you never know, she said, oh, and one more thing love.

She glanced around.

It always rains on a Thursday, she said.

Fair enough. The fact that it wasn't raining and it wasn't Thursday didn't seem to bother her.

And then she was gone, lost in the crowd, a harmless, slightly bonkers old lady who just wanted to talk to someone. It just turned out that that someone was me, because it always is.

Up by the Town Hall there used to be an ugly building that the locals called the *Egg Box*. It's been pulled down now because, well, it looked like an egg box, which is as good a reason as any. In its place are the Peace Gardens. The Peace Gardens has two things going for it. One, it's full of high-tech, super-duper water features, and two, it looks nothing like an egg box. There are fountains and gullies and sprays and water jets that magically shoot up out of the ground. It's impressive, expensive and looks like a giant bidet. I was watching the water jet thingy thinking what a hoot it'd be to get drunk and naked and splash about getting wet and happy. I was about to dive in when I saw a sign saying *No Splashing About Getting Wet and Happy* or something like that. I put my trousers back on and stayed dry and miserable.

There were a couple of Japanese tourists milling about taking photos. They had at least three cameras each, pointed at things and laughed a lot. I sat and watched for a while. It's not every day you see real living and breathing stereotypes. They looked 30 years too late, like they'd walked straight out of a Benny Hill sketch. They had good smiles and bad glasses. They bowed at each other and wore loud checked jackets that made your eyes go funny. They even had comedy Japanese accents, full of little whoops and yells. I looked around. Maybe they were putting all this on just for me, giving me my own tasty little piece of eastern improv. Whatever they were doing it worked because after a while it was me who felt like the tourist. It was me who should have been snapping away and grinning. It was me who should have felt a long way from home.

And I did.

The white noise of the water was doing things to me, taking me out of myself. Peace Gardens? Come off it. It sounded like someone sandblasting the inside of my head. I couldn't hear myself think. But maybe that's the point, to learn to take a step back and switch off now and again. There is something Japanesey about the Peace Gardens, something purging and Oriental about the slush and gurgle of water and the wide openness of it all. Sheffield is Tokyo.

When I got out of the Peace Gardens my ears were ringing and I was all over the place. I didn't know where I was. I went into the Proper Pasty Company and asked for a custard flavoured bacon sandwich. I got a funny look so I bought a Cornish pasty flavoured Cornish pasty instead. I stood in front of the Town Hall to have a breather and get my bearings. I looked up to the left and saw Yorkshire House. I looked right and saw the Yorkshire Bank. Things were clicking into place. When I bit into my pasty it all became clear: Sheffield is Sheffield.

Seven o'Clock: Holme

The man with the moon face wasn't amused. I cracked my best funny about tractors and he was having none of it.

I used to like tractors, I said, but now I don't.

I paused for effect.

I'm an ex-tractor fan.

Nothing.

Moonface wasn't having it, not a bit.

The village of Holme sits at the northern end of the Holme Valley. In fact it doesn't as much sit as put its feet up, chill out and crack open a cold one. It's that kind of place. I stumbled into Holme on the day of the Annual Tractor Run. There were tractors all over the place: a splatter of tractors; a clutch of tractors; a belch of tractors?

They all hugged the middle of the road and they weren't shifting. Good looking David Browns, Nuffields, Fords and McCormicks, all done up in their Sunday best. Scrubbed up and gleaming in fire-engine red, lurid green and summersky blue. They looked like cartoons. These old boys were spic and span and hadn't come within a mile of a dung heap for years. You could taste the spit, the polish and the elbow grease. These were the classics, saved from the scrappers, and wheeled out for galas, shows and the Holme Annual Tractor Run. The drivers, like the tractors, seemed to belong to another era. The majority went for the Pop Larkin look: flat caps, check-shirts and waistcoats. They had big bellies and big smiles that sat on faces the colour of old cricket balls. Some even had passengers – wives that looked half-embarrassed. Others just had enough room for pets – dogs that looked completely embarrassed. Some went the whole hog and bounced about on tractors festooned with bunting, balloons and Union Jacks. These men became part of the tractors and it was hard to tell where the tractor stopped and the man started.

Every now and again you'd see tractors driven by putty-faced men. Accountants, recruitment consultants, call centre managers, you know the type. These men wore polo shirts and hundred quid sunglasses. They looked like they'd be more at home discussing incentive schemes and bollocking the idiot from the agency. Not that the tractors were bothered. As long as you give it plenty of oil, let it winter inside and go easy with the gearbox a 1945 Massey-Ferguson is a good friend to anybody.

The best thing about Holme is its name. Holme was obviously someone's home at one time so they called it Holme. Stands to reason. Drive through Holme and you come to a place called Lane Village. Lane Village is a village with a lane running through it. No pubs, shops or churches to clutter up the place. I reckon if you keep driving round Holme for long enough you'll find places called Tree, Pond, Hill and Field. Simple really. Although why Holme is twinned with a trumped up place called Canton D'Imply is anyone's guess.

On the road into Holme you pass the Holme Castle Hotel. This looks like the kind of place where people with a few quid meet to compare tans and flirt over champagne cocktails. It stands opposite the 17th century Sunday School on Field Head Lane. The field itself was full of cows. I clapped and mooed for a while to attract some attention.

I failed.

The best I got was a look that said – *We are cows, what do you want from us?* At the end of Field Head Lane is Digley reservoir, in fact Holme has to be the reservoir capital of the world. In an area covering one square mile you'll find Digley, Bilberry, Brownhill, Ramsden, Ridley Wood and Yateholme reservoirs. The people of Holme should smile and drink deep. They'll never get thirsty.

When I saw a place called Good Bent I knew I had to go, I just *had* to. Good Bent is at the end of Digley reservoir and leads down to Good Bent End and on to Good Bent Lodge. Do you know how hard it is for someone born in the 60s who grew up on a televisual diet of Frankie Howerd, The Carry Ons and Mrs Slocombe's pussy not to make lewd jokes about places like Good Bent End? I have to keep biting my lip. In my own little world Good Bent Lodge would be the place where Sid James laughs his diesel and whiskey laugh while Barbara Windsor wobbles about in a bikini two sizes too small. Kenneth Williams would flare his nostrils and go *Oooo Matron* and

Frankie Howerd would look on warning us *not to titter.* In reality Good Bent is just a patch of scrub that slopes down to a reservoir. Not a titter in sight. Sometimes being in your own little world is the best place to be.

The Fleece is a good-looking stone-built pub on the main road through Holme. Outside the pub is a sign saying *Good Beer* and *Fine Home Cooked Food.* Shouldn't that be *Holme* cooked food, I think they missed a chance there. It also has good views of Netherley Brow, High Brow and the public toilets. I'm sat in the Fleece thinking about tractors when the man with the moon face walked in. He ordered a John Smith's and sat next to me.

A good day for tractors, he said.

I nodded.

Moonface took a sup and sighed. It was a sigh that said life is sweet and the beer is sweeter.

You a tractor man then? he asked.

I was ready for him.

I used to like tractors but now I don't,

I paused for effect, then, I let him have it.

I'm an ex-tractor fan, I said.

Moonface sat for a while, looked at me like the cows did, then sloped off to find another seat.

Eight o'Clock: Portsmouth

It was weather for ducks.

Big ducks.

The sky was a dishcloth and the big man upstairs was wringing it out. The windscreen wipers were struggling to cope and looked ready to throw in the towel. The radio buzzed, died and buzzed again. I kept rolling. I was going to Portsmouth. That's Portsmouth the Yorkshire version, not Portsmouth the look-at-me-I'm-famous Hampshire version. It was actually *that* Portsmouth where Walter Raleigh brought back the first spuds and tobacco from the New World. The next time you have a wheeze on a Silk Cut and polish off a chip butty, spare a thought for good old Wally. Cancer and cholesterol. What a legacy.

Portsmouth is on the border of Yorkshire and Lancashire. Drive through it and you drive into another book called *Lancashire in a Crombie*. I'll leave that one to Peter Kay. On the main road is a pub called the Glen View Hotel. I licked my lips. Carlsberg, Stella, Heineken, anything fizzy and European sounded good. It was a bit worrying. It was eight in the morning.

So why is Portsmouth called Portsmouth? What's that all about? It has neither port nor mouth. Maybe an old seadog, scurvy-scarred and rum-soaked, decided that his days of shivering his timbers and splicing his main-brace were numbered and dropped anchor there? Maybe a fast-fingered, granite jawed Navy captain dealt off the bottom and won this patch of land in a rigged game of poker? Maybe a clueless town planner couldn't be arsed and threw a dart at a map of England? It doesn't matter, Portsmouth is called Portsmouth. Full stop.

Two old ladies were stood in the bus shelter waiting for the number 92 to Todmorden. They were talking about the weather. I couldn't hear them but I didn't need to. The glum looks, the shaking heads, the sighing. Who needs words? They were talking about the weather alright.

Across the road from the bus shelter was a steep sided conifer wood. It looked like someone had been to Austria on their jollies, dug up a piece of the Alps and smuggled it back through Customs. If I closed my eyes and looked hard enough I could see the Von Trapps skipping through the trees belting out *The Hills are Alive*.

With the sound of music.

Bloody hell. I really did need a drink.

The rain was enjoying itself. It had rolled its sleeves up and gotten heavier. Ah well. You know what they say, there's no such thing as bad weather, only the wrong clothes. Outside the mini-market the gutter was running away with itself and the Busy Lizzies in the hanging baskets didn't look that busy.

Then suddenly, without warning, my heart broke.

There was a dog tied up outside the shop. It was a spaniel, I'm not sure what kind, Uncle Jim would have known. It had big eyes and long ears. It looked me in the eye. I looked back. I didn't blink. I didn't breathe. I didn't feel the rain. I was staring at the saddest face I'd ever seen. Think of all the saddest songs you've ever heard: *Seasons in the Sun, Vincent, Grocer Jack, Two Little Boys*. Roll them all up into one bigweepy ball and they don't even come close. The dog just sat there getting wetter and wetter. I stood there forever. The Crombie got heavier and heavier. Then a bloke with a not-bothered face and a blue Berghaus top came out of the mini-market, untied the dog and walked him up the road. That was it, moment over. But it wasn't, not for me. I wanted to do something. I wanted to jump in the puddles, get soaked to the skin and sod the world. I wanted to run home in the rain and write a blues song. I wanted to dig one up from that place deep behind my heart. I needed, *needed*, to feel that dog's pain. I stood there forever again.

I went back to the Glen View Hotel. It was still closed. As I drove out of Portsmouth I was spitting feathers but I knew one thing: the Glen View Hotel is the best pub I've never been in. Driving back through Todmorden I pass the Bent Burger takeaway and look up. The Stoodley Pike Crimean War monument ignored the rain and stood to attention high on the hill. I threw a cheesy salute back at it. Down the road a mile and I pass a pub called WANWOECKS. I like the sound of that; kind of tribal and Aboriginal. I've seen those blokes on the Discovery Channel supping sap from gum trees, squirting the juice from frogs down each other's throats. I liked what I saw. I pulled up. The landlord put me straight. The pub was really called the Swan With Two Necks. The rain had washed half the sign away. A bloke was coming to fix it next Wednesday. Not to worry. I'd have to make do with Carlsberg. The sap and the frog juice would just have to wait.

Nine o'Clock: Wigglesworth

The A65 Ilkley to Kirby Lonsdale road is tailor-made for car chases. It's twisty and turny and has plenty of blind corners and narrow bridges. The cops and robbers shows that had me glued to the box when I was growing up would have loved it. I can imagine Bodie and Doyle from *The Professionals*, squealing round tight right-handers and speeding through Skipton and Gargrave, paper and cardboard boxes flying all over the place. They'd have some fisticuffs with the bad guy and batter a confession out of him. Then they'd chat the barmaid up in the Black Horse in Hellifield before Cowley comes in and gives them a rollicking – *Doyle, get yer haircut lad.* I can see *The Sweeney's* Jack Regan tucked behind the wheel of a growling 3-litre Capri. He's wearing Ron Atkinson's old sheepskin coat and he's doing the 3 S's:

1. Smoking.
2. Scowling.
3. Swearing.

Especially the last one. Bloody this and bloody that and bloody everything in-between. The crafty baddie would try to shake him and throw a quick right at Long Preston. Regan would do a handbrake turn and get stuck behind a muckspreader.

Bloodybloodybloody.

Then he'd double back and burn some serious rubber all the way to Giggleswick before finally nailing his man in the Ye Olde Naked Man café in Settle. He'd walk in, scowl a bit, stub his Lambert and Butler Kingsize out on the bad guy's Danish pastry and say – *Finish your tea son, you're nicked.*

Bloody right he would.

In Wigglesworth everything is something else. Nothing is really sure what it's supposed to be. On the village sign there is a white rose and a red one. The Lancashire border and the Forest of Bowland are about two miles away. I reckon it's make-your-mind-up-time. The Post Office is a general store, the petrol station is a car lot and the pub doubles as a restaurant. That's multi-tasking for you. It all started when bus drivers suddenly became bus conductors. That's how I look at it anyway. When things go pear-shaped, blame the buses. You won't be far wrong.

There is a sign on the Post Office window:

Please leave your dogs and horses outside. Hooks and rings provided.

That's right. Horses. I don't think they were joking.

Wigglesworth doesn't have a church, it shares one with Rathmell up the road, and the village itself is dominated by its only pub. No church but a big old boozer, sounds about right. Who needs the Lord when you've got John Smith's? The Plough looks like the kind of place Dick Turpin would have pulled in to polish his pistol and water Black Bess. No multi-tasking for Dick. He was strictly a one-man, one-job sort of bloke. The Plough has shiny trophies and photos of a smug darts team on show behind the bar. There are framed certificates on the wall telling me how clever-clever the quiz team are. When it comes to food the menu has a touch of the Jamie Oliver's about it. How does the Barbary Duck served on a bed of Spinach with Blackcurrant and Liquorice Sauce sound to you? Sounds like a lot of work to me, way too much prep. Why bother anyway when the darts team would be happy with Pie and Peas? I put the menu down and ask the barman for a bag of cheese and onion crisps.

Sorry, he says, fresh out.

Fresh out?

Fresh out.

He looks straight at me. I look straight back. For some reason I feel like saying sorry to him. I don't know why.

We have plain, salt and vinegar, he says, Worcester sauce and prawn cocktail.

But no cheese and onion?

No cheese and onion.

He looks at me again.

I nearly say sorry again.

We have peanuts, he says, dry roasted.

I don't want peanuts I say to myself.

Peanuts will do fine, I say to the barman.

Bugger, I should have gone for the duck.

There is a white haired lady hunched in the corner doing a

crossword. I bet she's the one who polished off all the cheese and onion. She has a glassy look and sighs a lot. Big, breathy, desperate sighs. Either she's having an off day or that crossword's a bit on the tricky side. I left her to it and took my peanuts outside.

The best thing about Wigglesworth is where it is. Everything seems far away, like squinting through the wrong end of the telescope. The land behind the Plough is a watercolour full of nothing but light, space and feathery brushstrokes. The Ribble Valley unfolded in front of me like a big picnic blanket. In the distance I could make out the salt and pepper peaks of Pen-y-gent and Ingleton.

I made a wish.

A proper one, I closed my eyes, counted to ten and everything. I know the rules.

I wished, really wished, that I was sat on top of one of those big old hills, eating soggy ham butties and drinking stewed tea out of a cheap flask.

But I'm not.

I'm here in Wigglesworth eating peanuts I didn't want and listening to old ladies sighing. I'm doing it because that's how it is. I'm doing it because that's what you do when nothing else matters and your life comes down to 8 down and 6 across.

Poor soul, serves her right for eating all the crisps.

Ten o'Clock: Hawes

I'm in Laura's Cottage Tea Shop in Hawes. There are net curtains on the windows and a stuffed toy lion on a shelf. Why? I don't know and I'm not going to ask. I've gone for the orange cake, made with real oranges, and a cup of tea made with real tea. The waiter who serves me is the spit of Frank Carson.

There you go my friend, he says.

Cheers Frank, I say back. I ignore the funny look.

Outside Laura's a coach-load of pensioners rolls up. The driver brakes, opens the doors and lights a fag up *at the same time*; they must learn that at driving school. Back on the coach there was a lot of good quality stretching, head scratching and general wakey-up-ness going on but the yawning was in a different league, real world class stuff. Watching it was hypnotic. I could feel myself going under, slipping deeper and deeper. I didn't know pensioners had such big mouths.

Old people eh?

It was Dad talking. He'd come along for the ride.

They're stuck for summat to do aren't they? I mean take your Auntie Pam, she's started at night school now, doing computers. What for eh? I mean what's she gonna do with that? She's over the moon because she can pay her gas bill on the computer. She'll never leave the house.

Dad shook his head.

I knew this fella, he said, who retired and went to live in a bungalow in Filey and y'know what they said eh?

It was my turn to shake my head.

They said that when he got there, he forgot what he'd gone for.

Dad eyed up my orange cake.

Are you eating that? he said.

I let him have it.

He took a bite.

Anyway, he said, with his mouth full, you know what happens to you when you live in a bungalow don't yer?

What?

Dad swallowed my cake.

Bungalow legs, he said.

Bungalow legs?

Dad nodded.

Oh aye, all your muscles in your legs wither away to nowt cos you don't use em anymore to go up the stairs. There was summat about it in the *Courier* t'other day. Old people are sat there on computers and they've got no muscles in their legs.

Dad shook his head again.

I mean what the bloody hell, he said.

Yeah, I said, what the bloody hell.

I left Dad with my cake and went for a mooch around Hawes. My mooch is somewhere between a stroll and a ramble, kind of a strooch or a mamble. Strooch and Mamble? There's a cop show in there somewhere. First stop was the Parish Church. I sat on a bench with a plaque saying *Best Kept Village 1994*. I don't know what's happened since. Maybe they've stopped trying. I bet there's another bench somewhere with *We Really Can't Be Bothered Anymore* written on it. The graveyard was neat and tidy but dead people always are. You don't see dead people throwing crisp packets all over the place or flicking sparking fag-ends out of car windows. Well not in Hawes anyway. One headstone caught my eye. It read *The Late Clement Scott 1858*. I liked that, especially the *Late* bit, it smacks of somebody trying too hard. The fact that his name has 1858 written after it and it's carved on a tombstone in a graveyard full of graves tells me all I need to know about poor old Clement. By the church gate was an old milk churn that's been slotted and made into a big money box. On top of it was a handwritten sign:

Will you please help us raise £250,000 for essential repairs.

Opposite the church is the Hawes branch of the HSBC. Well there you go, forget the milk churn. All God has to do is have a quiet word with the bank manager. I can't see any problems. Anyone who can create the world in six days should get a decent credit rating.

On the main street in Hawes is the best shop in the world. It's called *John Hogg Chemist and Wine and Spirit Merchant*. Mr Hogg is a man who clearly knows how the world works. Well, my world at least. You can go into his shop, buy a bottle or two for the night before and a box of paracetamol for the morning after. Now that's what you call service. He should get a knighthood.

Arise Sir Hogg of Hawes.

Alright it sounds like a villain out of *The Wind In The Willows* but the tourists would lap it up. In Hogg's window is a selection of Yorkshire County Wines. We're talking real wine here, the kind made from Rhubarb, Damson, Cherry, Gooseberry and Elderflower not those soft Mediterranean ones made out of grapes. Who needs those? Hogg's also sells Black Sheep Beer. I bought a bottle. It's hoppy with a kick and smells like it was made this morning. It comes with the slogan:

Take a little bit of Yorkshire *baaa...ck* home with ewe.

Now you want to be careful there. You get into sheep jokes and you can find yourself on dodgy ground very quickly. One minute you're innocently going *baa...ck* with ewe, and the next you're getting into graphics and talking about wellies and shearing. Believe me, sheep gags are best left alone.

I did the touristy bit and bought a Yorkshire tea-towel. On the front was a little squiggly map of the biggest county and all the usual suspects, York Minster, Ripon Cathedral, Whitby Harbour and the castles of Richmond, Skipton and Helmsley. On the back was a Made in Pakistan label. That did it for me. We can knock out churches and castles by the cartload but tea-towels? Forget it.

I walked down to the river, crossed the bridge and passed the Hawes Club. No messing there. This is Hawes and this is our Club. We do what we do. Like it or lump it. I liked it, it's direct, blunt and to the point. It could be the Yorkshireness I've been looking for. I even thought about joining up. For a quid a week you can be a Casual Member. Sounds like a bargain. If you want to be a Really Intense Member, that'll cost a bit more. I stood on the bridge and practised being casual for a bit. I think I'm a natural.

The river was making a lot of noise. It sounded like it had just come back from somewhere really exciting and wanted to tell everybody about it. I had a sneaky peek in the Three Peaks outdoor shop with its window full of Gore-Tex, SympaTex, This-Tex and That-Tex walking boots. I'm OK on the boot front so I bought a Thinsulate fleece hat and mooched back to base-camp Laura's with a warm head.

Eleven o' Clock: Richmond

It's Richmond and the sky has forgotten what colour it's supposed to be. It's wet cement and wallpaper paste, it's wood smoke and tramp's teeth, it's the fluffydusty stuff that comes out of the Hoover bag, it's that lagging that you get on old boilers.

JMW Turner, the landscape artist, was shacked up in Richmond for a while. He'd have been easy to spot. He'd be the one moping around town looking all tortured and misunderstood. They used to call Turner, the painter of light. I could have done with him today. He could have splashed some sun across the sky.

I remember speaking to Jesus, not *the* Jesus, the Son of God variety, but the little-bald-bloke-from-Barcelona-I-used-to-work-with version. Jesus came over to live in Leeds. I asked him how he liked the place.

I like very much how one minute you are in the city and the next in the country, he said.

Is there anything you miss about home? I asked him.

He looked at me and nodded.

El llum, he said, I miss the light.

It's a good job Jesus wasn't with me in Richmond. He'd have crossed himself, jumped in the river and never been seen again.

No me toques los cojones, he'd have said.

You'll have to look that one up.

Richmond is posh. I know that because jacket spuds cost a fiver and when people bump into you they do that posh apology thing.

Ever so sorry, they say, ever so.

It's not the sorry I have a problem with, that's fine, it's the *ever so* bit that gets to me. Sorry is a word that works on its own. It's a one-man band. It's been around a long time and gets people out of sticky situations. Put *ever so* in front of it though and all you do is over-egg the pudding. You end up sounding like you're not sorry at all. In fact you sound like you think I should be the one saying sorry to you for being stupid enough to allow you to bump into me in the first place. Have I gone off on one here?

Sorry.

I'm walking through Market Place, on my way to the river, when I pass two teenage girls. They were stood holding court in front of Boots. They were both smoking and looked like they meant what they were saying.

So I sez to her, one said, I sez mingin bitch, yer can piss right off yer can.

Oh I know, the other said, cos I mean if she cart tek it then she shunt friggin dish it out.

Bitch.

Slapper.

Gobby cow.

That cheered me up. Suddenly I felt at home.

Somebody told me that now and again, if your luck's in, you might spot a swan on the river in Richmond. I wanted to see one, if only so I could say – *How sweetly the swan swims on the swirling Swale.* Now there's a line you could get lost in. I'm going to say it again, just for the hell of it - *How sweetly the swan swims on the swirling Swale.* It's even better a second time. I had a quick shufty at the water but the swan was a no show. Fair enough. Life was never meant to be a tongue twister.

Richmond is Malton on steroids. It's Grassington without the grass. It's Skipton without the skip. It is, according to the tourist blurb – *Britain's best kept secret...*

And there they go again, over doing it. Those three little dots after secret means that they're not finished, there's something else to follow. It's also an open invitation for you to find out exactly what that *something* is. They're playing games with you. Don't fall for it. Besides, it's wrong anyway. Best kept secret? Richmond is such a secret that I couldn't find a parking place. The world and its mother had come for the day. I finally found a place to park in front of Barker's Traditional Fish and Chip shop. Next to me was a mucky transit with SINGLE WHITE VAN SEEKS SPONGE FOR GOOD CLEAN FUN written on it. When I went into Barker's and asked for a bag of chips, the bloke told me they had none left.

Ever so sorry, he said.

Don't you bloody start, I thought.

I was going to have a go at him but he gave me a Shrek fridge magnet so I let him off.

Thanks, I said, ever so.

Hey, when in Rome.

I bought a Yorkshire curd tart from Thomas the Baker and had a flick through *The Advertiser*. On the front page was the headline – FREE SAUSAGE ROLLS FOR EVERY READER. Now there's an idea. Maybe I should put that on the front of this book. That should shift a few copies.

At the top of Market Square is a big stone needletype thing. I asked a bloke in a Leeds Rhinos shirt if he knew what it was called.

Does this obelisk have a name? I asked.

Yeah, he said with a smirk, it's called an obelisk.

I nearly stuck my curd tart in his face.

I was standing at the top of Finkle Street looking at Richmond laid out in front of me. I could see Trinity Church and the Green Howards Museum, I could see The Bishop Blaize pub with its Roy Castle Fresh Air Award certificate stuck in the window. I could see the Castle flag flying and tea rooms next door to tea rooms. I could see it all. Richmond feels like a full size model village. It has a Legoland meets Fisher Price quality to it. I think it's the Castle's fault and the way everything is plonked round the cobbled Market Square. You can imagine big hands coming out of the sky and moving things about. The place names don't help: Pottergate, Quaker Lane, Holly Hill. It's Fraggle Rock meets Trumpton meets Toytown. Finkle Street is the kind of street you can imagine Noddy and Big Ears walking down on their way for a swift one in the King's Head Hotel.

I finished my curd tart and looked around. Richmond has its own feel. It's old and it's new. It's blue-less skies and swan-less rivers. It's five quid jacket spuds and gobby cows. Whatever you say about Richmond, it's very Richmondy.

Ever so.

Twelve o'Clock: Potto

It's Potto and it's the top of the clock. I went to Potto for three reasons:

1. I've never been.
2. It ends in O.
3. It sounds like something out of *Lord Of The Rings.*

You know the type: one part Elf, one part Jimmy Krankie; don't worry, I won't say fandabbydozie.

Oops.

The sign said Potto 2 miles. Two miles further on I passed another sign that said the same thing. Either someone's taking the whatsit or I'm stuck in a cheap science fiction novel. That's the thing about the A19, turn off it and the rule book goes out of the window, space and time begin to melt and merge. Miles don't mean anything, the map you have in front of you might as well be behind you and tractors drive on whichever side of the road they bloody well want to. Oh yes.

I kept circling the earth until I came across another sign that said Potto ½ mile. I was getting warm. I knew I was close because all the houses had names like Potto Grange, Potto Fields Farm and Potto Hall. I thought about my mate who wanted to call his house Wits End but the Post Office wouldn't let him. They said it wasn't in keeping with the area. I wouldn't mind but his neighbour's house was called Old Knob.

Best move on.

The first thing I noticed about Potto was the noise, the hum, thrum and buzz of it. All I could hear were lawnmowers, hedge-trimmers and strimmers. Maybe it was International Garden Week or maybe the Queen was popping in later for a brew, I don't know. All I know is that people were getting busy. An old bloke was messing about with a hanging basket. He was doing his best and ignoring his wife who was shaking her head and telling him how he was doing everything wrong. Another bloke was standing on a wobbly chair trimming a wobbly hedge with some wobbly shears. Two gardens down a middle-aged woman was pruning her roses wearing yellow washing-up gloves. There was everything and nothing going on. Potto looked like one of those villages you see on *Midsomer Murders*. Everything is all tickety-boo for a while until one day the vicar goes bonkers and starts drugging people and clubbing them over the head in the vestry. The place was just too perfect.

Or maybe not.

One bloke wearing a trilby looked up from his Fly-Mo and gave me the once over. Then he took his trilby off and gave me the twice over. Then he turned off his lawnmower, put his trilby back on and pretended to be doing something else, all the time he just kept staring at me.

Staring and staring.

I don't know what I'd done. Maybe it was the Crombie he didn't like. I smiled at him but it didn't work. I shrugged, left him to it and checked out the public notice board. There was something about Swainby Aerobics Group and a notice reminding you that the bin collection day is changing during May Day Bank Holiday, all gripping stuff. Next to that was an article telling you that Potto Neighbourhood Watch is on the lookout for a man with a white van. He's in his mid-twenties with a moustache and has been going round offering to carry out house repairs. I looked over at my friend in the trilby. He was still doing it, staring and staring. I was lucky. If I'd have been in my mid-twenties with a tash, he'd probably have shot me.

At the top of Cooper Lane was a man on a horse. He looked at me. The horse looked at me. Neither of them smiled. Outside the church there was a young boy wearing a Dream Team football shirt and eating a big silly ice cream. He smiled but that didn't count. Kids eating big silly ice creams smile at anyone. I walked past the Dog and Gun. I could have used a drink but the place was still getting over the night before. On the wall was a sign saying AA APPROVED. I presume it meant the Automobile Association and not Alcoholics Anonymous. Now that's a sign you'd want to see:

GET BLOTTO IN POTTO, THAT'S OUR MOTTO!

Now you're talking.

When I got back to the car the man in the trilby was still giving me the eye. When I opened the door and got in, I looked across at him. He took off his hat and smiled.

Goodbye, he said.

He'd been dying to say that to me all day.

I popped into Thirsk on the way back because I wanted to. Besides, any town with a racecourse and loads of pubs is fine by me. It was market day and time to snap up a bargain. One bloke had a stall that sold watches. He wore fat gold chains around his fat gold neck so I gave him a miss. Another bloke was a bath specialist and sold fluffy towels, robes and bottles of smellystuff with fancy names like *Desire, Sensuality* and *Le Homme.* Not for me, I'm more of a carbolic man myself. One stall sold bedding plants, razor blades, teabags, old cassettes, Yorkshire postcards and personalised pine toilet seats. If you ever want to get up in a morning, sit on your very own toilet seat, have a shave and plant a flower whilst having a brew, writing to a friend and listening to jazz then this is the stall for you. I was thinking about all this when the bloke asked me if I was interested in anything. I was going to buy a postcard but I live in Yorkshire so that would be cheating. I really fancied a loo seat with CB on it but I bottled it and went for a Louis Armstrong tape instead.

Baker's Alley in Thirsk gets its name after the famous botanist John Gilbert Baker 1834-1920. I know that because a plaque on the wall told me. Local boy Baker did well for himself and ended up as curator of the Royal Gardens at Kew. In his spare time he wrote a really important book called *Flora of North Yorkshire.* He also wrote some less important books called *Betty of West Yorkshire* and *Gladys of South Yorkshire.*

Time for a pint.

The Blacksmith's Arms at the top of Market Square is one of those low beamed ceilings, real fires and stone floor jobs. There is an anvil in the corner and 1940s *Classic* cigar posters all over the walls. The jukebox makes the right noises and the beer knows what it's doing. From the window in the front lounge you have a great view of the Golden Fleece across the square and the Black Bull across the road. You can sit there all day and plan where to go for your next pint. Or you can just sit there all day.

At the next table there is a young couple. They were sharing a bottle of wine and doing that lovey-dovey-staring-at-each-other-without-speaking thing. Love has its own language. The man had a sip of wine and leaned in close towards to the woman.

You know what I like about you, he said.

The woman smiled.

Tell me, she whispered.

The man grabbed hold of her hand and gently stroked the back of it.

Your big fat arse, he said.

Who said romance was dead.

I left the young lovers to it, went outside and parked myself on the steps of the clock-tower. Above me was a big cloud shaped like a cow's head. It had a nose and ears and everything. Around me people were sitting on benches eating fish and chips from the White Horse Café and wolfing down jacket spuds from the Crusty Cob. I was hungry just sitting there. The clock-tower itself was erected by public subscription to commemorate the marriage of HRH The Duke of York and HRH The Princess Mary of Teck in 1896. Teck? Where the hell's that? I think they made it up. From where I was sat I could see the Yorkshire Sweet Stall in the market, the Yorkshire Deals discount shop, the Yorkshire Bank and the White Rose bookshop. That's the thing about Thirsk, there's Yorkshire everywhere.

I knew it was time to make tracks when the cow-shaped cloud broke up and floated away. I walked back to the car, took the Crombie off and got in. There was only one thing left to do. I got out my tape, clicked it on and let Louis Armstrong sing me home.

Pocket Size

Welcome

Welcome to Yorkshire. Now sod off.

Written on the back of a toilet door in Leeds/Bradford Airport:

The Pennines are Reg Sykes

I was born in Halifax in the 60s in a council house that got knocked down in the 70s. I went to a school in the 70s that got wrecking-balled in the 80s. I have to keep moving or I'll get condemned. I popped out in the front room while *Come Dancing* was on. Mum used to say that I danced my way into this world. I was born in Yorkshire, but only just. Our house was closer to Oldham than Harrogate, as the crow flies, closer to Manchester than York. If it wasn't for the Pennines I'd be living in *Coronation Street*, getting off my face on Newton and Ridley's and punching Mike Baldwin. I'd have a Manc-twang and say things like – *Do you not want a cup of tea do you not?* I'd have gone to the Hacienda, dropped some E's with Shaun Ryder and grooved all night to the Stone Roses. Noel Gallagher would be from my neck of the woods and I'd call Liam *Our kid*. I'd be mad for it if it wasn't for the Pennines.

To me the Pennines are a landscape in limbo. They're not pretty in a postcardy, Lake Districty kind of way and they're not as big as some of their Scottish cousins. The Pennines dither about under clouds that dither back. They look half-finished, as if the bloke who put them there got rained off, went to the pub and forgot to come back.

To understand the Pennines you've got to introduce yourself to them. You've got to get out there, up on the hills, and put one foot in front of the other, left, right, left, right, your heartbeat thumpthumping in your head. I like to listen to it. It's good to know I'm still alive.

I remember watching a bloke hang-gliding over Buckstones Edge above Huddersfield. He told me about his mate who went up to 17,000 feet, passed out and came to on the way down. When I asked him what it was like up there, he just looked at me and smiled.

Like disappearing, he said.

I know what he means. Walking gets me like that. When you're out there walking, and everything's working, it's like you're not there. It's like you're sitting at home with your feet up watching repeats of *The Rockford Files*. I'm not talking about hiking and retired geography teachers with goatees, mincing about with waterproof maps hanging around their necks. The crowd who give you the daggers because you haven't got your £80 trousers tucked into your £300 fuel-injected, turbo-charged, walking boots. The Berghaus brigade who struggle from the 4x4 to the tea shop before making the big push to the tourist information centre for a postcard and box of Auntie Bessie's mass-produced homemade fudge. I'm talking about real walking, about just doing it and letting your body and your mind wander.

It is nice fudge though.

The Pennines are menacing, unfriendly and bleak. Call them ugly if you like, see if they care. It all comes down to character. The Pennines are a drug dealer you owe big style, a nasty piece of work called Frankie who has a finger missing and picks his gold teeth with a flick knife. They're the taxman, the rent man and the county court bailiff all rolled into one. They're anyone who earns a living looking grim and not smiling. They're a grizzly old bloke who lives on his own, kicks cats and eats cold beans out of a can. The Pennines are Reg Sykes who lived up our road. He'd shout at the ice cream man if he parked in front of his house, kick seven bells out of his van and accuse him of blocking his light.

Blocking his light.

Then he'd shout at us saying - *Get up yer own end* - and - *I know yer Father.* When we got him really wound up he'd start panting, get all red-faced and gaspy – *I'll stick a knife through that bloody football if it comes near my roses again. You watch me.* We watched him. He tried it once. He had one of those fancy Swiss Army jobs. He fumbled and fumbled but couldn't find the knife bit so he started stabbing the ball with a nail file.

Stabstabstab.

It didn't work so he had a go with the bottle opener, the pointy thing for getting stones out of horses' hooves, and the little scissors. The ball was having none of it. Reg sneered at us and gave it up as a bad job. They don't make balls like that anymore.

Talking about Reg's roses, why is Yorkshire's symbol a white rose? What's that all about? The history books say that Yorkshire soldiers picked white roses to commemorate fallen comrades after a punch-up in Minden, Germany in 1759. But surely that's the poppy's job? Maybe the poppy and the rose are doing a job-share. The white rose itself is a touch on the bland side. White is just a meaningless shade, a blank canvas. It's not even a proper grown-up colour. It's in league with grey and black, staying up late drinking cheap whisky and smoking roll-ups. Planning and plotting. All this monochromic canoodling makes the white rose a weird choice for a county that bangs on and on and on, and on some more, about its colourful landscapes and even more colourful characters. Blue is a real colour, so what about the bluebell, nodding its head and chuckling in the wind. Or we could go for the buttercup with its big cheesy grin or the dandelion's sunshine smile. Why not? They'd be more like it. Like huge chunks of Yorkshire itself, these flowers are wild, beautiful and free. They're not caged, cultivated and sold in pots at B&Q. Like the Pennines they do what they do and make it look easy.

The Pennines made me who I am. They put Yorkshire where it is. They keep it grounded, geographically and culturally, and stop it getting too big for its boots.

And Mum, if you can hear me, I'm still dancing.

A Million Pounds a Mile

Uncle Fred was a gardener for Halifax Borough Council. He knew his daffs from his dahlias, his hyacinths from his hybrids and his begonias from his bluebells. As a gardener he was good. The job kept his head above water and the wolf from the door. As a bodybuilder though, he was better than good. He won prizes. His mantelpiece was stuffed with cups, shields and trophies. One silver shield had *Yorkshire Lightweight Champion 1964* engraved on it.

Uncle Fred was a bit of a show-off and had a good party piece. He'd take his shirt off and flex his muscles. He had muscles everywhere: his back, his legs, his arms, even his arse looked strong. All the time he'd be singing his little strongman song. No words just *Dum-de-dum-de-dum-dum-diddle-iddle-dum-de-dum*. Then he'd put his finger in his mouth, blow and his bicep would balloon. I'd make him do it again and again. I was looking for clues, but I couldn't find any. He'd spark up a cig and lift a 56lb weight above his head with his little finger. Then he'd blow smoke rings, perfect smokeblue halos. He looked like *The Saint*. Dad couldn't do it, he'd get the weight so far, start shaking and give up. It was down to me. I thought if I kept listening to Mum, ate all my dinners and grow big then I'd be able to do it. Well that was 30 years ago and I'm all dinnered out. I tried the 56lb with the little finger yesterday. I couldn't shift it. I tried again, still no joy. One last go.

Dum-de-dum-de-dum-dum-diddle-iddle-dum-de-dum.

It didn't budge. All those dinners weren't working. I couldn't even blow the smoke rings. I had to face it. I'm no Uncle Fred

When Uncle Fred had enough of flexing he upped sticks and took

Auntie Dulce to Australia. He left Dad the 56lb weight and the keys to his cherry-red Oxford Morris. The Oxford Morris was a good looking motor, all chrome bumpers and shiny hubcaps. It looked like a car that would get you there and back with knobs on. Dad asked me and my brother if we fancied taking it for a drive.

Where to? Mark asked.

The M62, Dad answered.

I had no idea what the M62 was. It sounded strange and scientific, like something out of *Doctor Who* or *Thunderbirds*.

Brillo, I said, let's go.

Dad did 100mph that day. He hit the motorway and took off. I remember watching the speedo needle quivering its way up the dial. When it finally hit 100 we all cheered. I don't know why. No-one told us to. We just did. Dad, Mark and me shouting ourselves daft at the Big One Double-O. I watched as Dad put his foot down and his knuckles turned white on the steering wheel.

It cost a million pounds a mile to build this road, he said, and look at us eh, one hundred miles an hour at a million pounds a mile. Now we're motoring lads.

And we were.

I looked at Dad's eyes in the mirror. I could see the wrinkles at the corners. I knew he was smiling. Marko was laughing and snorting like a pig.

That's a ton up, he kept shouting, a ton up.

I was in the back. The seat was as big as my bed and it was all mine, every single inch of it. I was lording it up as the world blurred by at 100 miles an hour.

I remember thinking so this is what men do, this is what it feels like. I'd played football before, three-and-in, goalie-when-needed, champs and keepy uppy. I'd played British Bulldogs, kerbie and pile-on. I'd gone to Bolton Abbey on my bike, *on my own*. I'd even seen Julie Bennett with no knickers on.

Twice.

But tearing down the M62 at 100mph in a cherry-red Oxford Morris with your Dad and your big brother was a different kettle of testosterone. This, I thought to myself, was man's stuff.

The route for the M62 was finally decided in 1964 which pretty much makes me and the motorway the same age. The M62 looks good though, it's weathered better than I have. I'm a bit tatty round the edges, parts of me could do with being coned off and resurfaced. The M62 is a road that comes with its own history, its own mythology. I grew up listening to stories of a mad-as-a-hatter farmer who lived directly in the path of the motorway. This guy was a serious fruitcake who barricaded himself into his house and pointed his trusty twelve-bore at anybody who came within a stonesthrow. This was epic stuff, a story that got better with every telling - the fish just kept on getting bigger and bigger. It had everything. It was David against Goliath, one man against the government. It was Guy Fawkes all over again, real Yorkshire blood and guts. There were stories doing the rounds about booby-trapped diggers, dynamite strapped to diesel tanks and guns going off. This story even had a fairytale ending. The farmer won the battle and they had to build the motorway round him. What a result. Stott Hall Farm is still there, it's been there since 1738. You'll find it below High Moss between Junction 23 and 22. I remember Dad laughing and saying daft bugger, it'd only happen in Yorkshire.

The thing is though it didn't happen at all.

The mad-as-a-hatter farmer was Ken Wild, whose name was a gift for the headline writers. Imagine the front pages: *The Wild Man of the Moors; Wild by Name, Wild by Nature; Wild Thing.* But Ken didn't live up to his name, he was just a normal farmer doing normal farmer-type things with tractors and sheep. Because of a natural geological fault in the rock it was easier - and cheaper - to leave Ken's farm where it was and build the motorway around him. So that's exactly what they did. No booby traps, no guns going off, no nothing. What a bummer.

Enter Wilf Dyson.

Every myth has to start somewhere and I reckon Wilf is to blame for this one. When they flooded Scammonden to make the dam Wilf wasn't best pleased. Oh no. He'd farmed there all his life, just like his Dad and his Dad before him. We're talking lots of Dads here. Wilf, who looked like a cross between Catweazel and Yosemite Sam, threw his weight about a bit, told people to sod off and to generally leave his land alone. No-one listened. Wilf was just a crazy old man, what could he do?

This is what he did.

One morning there was a handwritten note stabbed to the site office door. It was held there by a blood stained dagger. Scrawled on the note was the message: *Get your devil diggers off my land or this'll happen to you.* Scary stuff. Wilf was angry, the worst kind of angry. He had nothing and everything to lose. He'd made his point. The note made the drivers, the drillers, the devil-diggers, the dynamiters and the top brass a bit edgy. Everyone looked over their shoulders for a while. But the motorway was bigger than Wilf, the job had to go on. They flooded Scammonden, built the dam and the M62 crossed over the mountains. Exit Wilf. I feel for him. Whatever he was, the man had style.

A few miles past Stott Hall Farm, just before the white rose turns red, the M62 goes up hill. At 1,221 feet above sea level it's the highest motorway in Britain.

Think about it.

That's five times as high as York Minster or twice as high as the Humber Bridge. Either way it's in the sky. To build it they used monster Russian trucks and Canadian snow-tractors. They looked like God's Tonka toys. Normal wagons just weren't up to the job. These foreign machines were tried and tested. They could handle the cold, the wind, the fog, the freezing diesel, and the freezing everything else. As for the rain, it does what it wants up there. It hits you in the face and slaps you on the back. It hurts you. One of the drillers said that the rain actually went up hill, *up hill.* He said it came out of nowhere and blew straight up his trouser leg. It all sounds a bit grim. Give me Wilf and his dagger any day.

Talking of things being grim, in 1991 a band called the Justified Ancients of Mu Mu got to number ten in the charts with a song called *It's Grim Up North.* It was one of those hypnotic songs with hardly any words and a bass-line that got into your head and went on forever. The song was good but needed a bit of zing to stand out, it needed a twist. The band twiddled their thumbs for a while before somebody came up with a bright idea.

Hey, somebody said, let's record some traffic on the motorway and add it to the mix.

Hey, somebody else said, let's do it.

It worked. Halfway through the song, the M62 made a guest appearance. It sounded good, kind of eerie. You could hear a horn in the distance and tyres sluicing on wet tarmac. I don't know how they did it but you could hear the fog as well. You really could. That was it for me. I was a fan.

I thought that the Justified Ancients Of Mu Mu were a top band. I wanted to find out more about them. It turned out they were just KLF messing about under a silly name. They might have been taking the mick but I wasn't bothered. How many other motorways do you know who have been on *Top of the Pops?*

I wanted to introduce myself to the M62. The motorway was like an old friend I'd relied on, taken for granted. I'd never really stopped, looked it in the eye and said hello. I'd never gone for a cuppa with it, shared in-jokes and laughed about old times. I'd sworn at it and got stroppy but it was always there. It got me where I was going and it got me home again. There's an old gag that the old club comics used that goes: *You know Yorkshire, it's where the M62 is cobbled.* Even though the motorway dips down into Lancashire it seems to be synonymous with Yorkshire. You can't think of one without thinking about the other. It belongs here. I'd been on the M62 countless times doing countless miles on countless days. But, like most people I'd always used it as the quickest way to get from A to B. I'd always been going somewhere. Well today it would be different, the motorway itself would be my A to B. Today the M62 would be my somewhere.

Let's lose the M for a start. Anyone who knows this road, *really* knows it, calls it the 62. So we will. Let's leave M to look after James Bond, we don't need him here.

Drive the Yorkshire stretch of the 62 and you not only undertake a geographical journey but a geological one. When you come over the Yorkshire-Lancashire border everything is on top of you: the rocks, the air you breathe, the sky. It's all a bit in-your-face. If this section of the motorway was in America, they'd invent a cool name for it like Heaven's Gate or the Devil's Drawbridge. It would be full of old hippies on Harleys trying to find themselves, man. Then again if the 62 was in America it wouldn't be called the 62 at all. It would be called the Trans-Pennine Express Super Highway. They'd even write a song about it, something along the lines of Route 66 but with different words.

And then it all gets a bit historical.

If you got a big dustpan and brush - and an even bigger bin-liner - and cleared away all the clutter at the side of the motorway: industrial estates, retail parks, Little Chefs, Total service stations, and all the rest of it, what you'd be left with is not just a road but a time machine that would transport you from prehistory to the present. Those slabs of millstone grit around Junction 22 somehow seem older than the wide open, flat marshlands of the East Riding Wolds. Maybe it's because you can see them, looming at you. You can slap them, carve your lover's name into them, become part of them. Maybe it's because, like the rings that run through old trees, you can see the age in them. It's right there in front of your eyes. When you drive past them you feel like you can stick your hand out of the window and touch them. They look computer generated, like the rocks in *Lord Of The Rings*. They're just too real, kind of ultra-physical. Or maybe it's just me being daft. Yeah, let's go with that.

God knows what people think when they come over the tops for the first time. They must feel like they're driving through an Ashley Jackson painting. There is nothing here and a lot of it. Look around. You could be on top of the world. You are 1,221 feet above sea level and you feel it. You're not driving, you're flying. Welcome to Moss Moor, the sticks, the Yorkshire outback. You've entered the Yorkshire of the mind. This is what Yorkshire looks like to people who have never been. Suddenly Betty's of Harrogate and Starbucks of Leeds seem a million miles away.

But they're not. At Junction 23 you drive straight back into the 21st century. Everything becomes familiar: houses, farms, pubs, electricity. On my left, a good stonesthrow away, is the village of Outlane. I had a mate Tony who holed up there for a while. He had a one-up, one-down tucked behind the Waggon and Horses. From his bedroom you could hear the 62 all night and all day. I asked him if the noise kept him awake. He shook his head.

There is an old Chinese proverb, he said, he who lives near the sea doesn't hear the waves.

Tony was always a bit odd.

But I know what he means. When the 62 is part of your everyday life then you have to deal with it. It becomes part of your inner-landscape, something you carry around. The white noise it makes becomes your own personal soundtrack. Then the 62 isn't the 62 anymore, it's just wallpaper.

It's just *there*.

Further along is the Calder Valley and the mill where Lord Gannex used to churn out raincoats for Harold Wilson. I cross the Calder, drive up the hill and pull in. It's time for a Welcome Break.

The car park at Hartshead Moor services is full of the usual: 4x4's, people carriers and minibuses. There was a BoozeBuster wagon and a mucky white transit van with JEFF IS SHIT AT GOLF scrawled on it. Lost people were shuffling about with AA Road Atlases and just-woken-up faces. They were saying things like *Is this Bradford?* and *Where the bloody hell has Sheffield gone?* I watched them for a while and thought about helping out but where's the fun in that? I left them to it and made my way to the GamesZone where the fruit machines live.

A bored security guard was tapping a text message into his mobile. He was away with the fairies. I could have backed a van in, emptied the room and he'd have been none the wiser. I threw a quid in the Play Till You Win Cranesaurus and played till I won. It paid off. I walked away with a fluffy pink dolphin.

I was on a roll.

After stumping up £3.85 for a Peppered Pastrami and Cheddar Cheese Panini I needed to sit down. I parked myself on a leather settee in front of a flat-screen TV and looked around. On the table next to me was a middle-aged couple. They weren't saying a lot but were making light work of a Burger King Whopper Meal. They looked like they'd been married forever.

And maybe that's the secret right there.

Stuff your face with a Whopper Burger and you *can't* talk, you just haven't got room in your mouth for any words, *and* if you can't talk then you can't argue and that's it, bingo, you'll live happily ever after. Next to them was a table of blokes who were all talking excitedly about Knutsford.

No really, they were.

Knutsford.

I think they deserve some kind of award.

Next to them was a gaggle of school kids all dressed in black combat pants and black jackets. They all had ghostly white faces and wore black skull and cross-bone caps. One had a T-shirt with *Call Me The Grim Reaper For I Am He* written on it. Either they'd just been to some Gothic outing or school uniforms have come on a bit. I was just about to introduce myself – *Hello Mr Reaper, what brings you here, not me I hope, ha ha ha* – when the man himself got up and ordered a large latte with a chocolate muffin on the side. Even Death, it seems, needs a sugar rush. Ah well. It was time for me and the dolphin to make tracks.

At Junction 26 is the M606, the road that connects Bradford to the 62 and the rest of the world. The M606 doesn't do much. It just goes in a pretty straight line for a couple of miles before giving up the ghost at Rooley Lane roundabout. Rooley Lane, along with Sticker Lane, Laisterdyke and Killinghall Road among others, all come together to form a kind of outer ring road, one that makes a bullseye out of Bradford.

Ring road.

Now there's a thing.

The words ring and road weren't meant to be bed-mates. The word *ring* sits alongside finger, worm and *a-ding-ding* and *road* teams up nicely with works, hog and *to Damascus,* no problem there, but when you put ring and road together you get trouble, heaps of it. For a start the phrase *ring road* is a lie. It's a nice sounding name for an ugly thing. A *ring road* should be a road strewn with rose petals. It should twinkle and be full of silver bells and cockleshells and pretty maids all in a row. A *ring road* should be made of cut-glass and make a nice *ping* sound when you flick it.

But they don't.

Ring roads don't *ping*. They don't twinkle and they go nowhere. All they do is go round and round and round, like a stupid dog chasing its tail. They're the modern equivalent of those stone walls the Romans used to build round cities. They keep the undesirables out and the desirables in. OK they're not as handy with the lead-shot and boiling tar as Caesar & Co, but basically, they do the same job.

In the good old days Junction 23 used to belong to Leeds, but now it has to share it with Ikea. I don't think it's too happy about it. You know it's Leeds because there's a big sign with the Royal Armouries, Tropical World and Harewood House written all over it. Then, like an afterthought, is a smaller sign with a football on it telling you how to get to Elland Road. Ikea are dragging their Swedish feet a bit and haven't got a road sign yet. It's only a matter of time. In fact I bet the design team are on the case right now. No prizes for guessing what it'll look like. It'll be blue and yellow, available in flat-pack and last for two minutes.

Gouranga is the word. You see it all over the place; on walls, sides of houses, backs of wagons, all tried and tested, classic graffiti hotspots. But Gouranga works best when you see it on motorway bridges. That's when it has real presence, like the one on the footbridge near Hartshead Moor. The word itself is some kind of Hare Krishna mantra meaning Be Happy. I don't know exactly what kind of god the Hare Krishnas worship but it must be a bloody good one to make you hang upside down over the 62 with nothing but a handful of posters and a bucket of wallpaper paste.

GOURANGA.

Now that's what you call Faith.

Get past the Leeds/Ikea turn off and things slow down. The 62 is getting into it and just letting things happen: Tingley roundabout, CarCraft, the M1, Asda, Scottish Courage, Wakefield Europort, the Aire and Calder Canal, you're in good hands here, the landscape knows what it's doing. It's been here before. It all goes swimmingly until you drive up to something that they call Drax.

And it's the perfect name for it.

Drax.

Drax really couldn't be anything else except what it is, an eyesore of cooling towers, chimneys and rusty pipes. This is Mr Burns' nuclear plant from *The Simpsons*. It's a space station. It's 1950s B-movie Russia all over again. It looks like something big has just landed or is getting ready to take off. It's the word Drax that does it, or, if you're into specifics, then it's the letter X that is to blame.

There's something not quite right about X, something slightly sinister and mysterious. Take the X away, turn Drax into *dram, drat* or *drab* and you lose all the nastiness in a single stroke. Put it back though and you're left with the Devil's dog or a Bond baddie.

If all the letters of the alphabet were lined up, side by side, in an ID parade then the smart money would be on X being the one singled out. It would be X having to stay behind and help the police with their enquiries. Oh, I know X can symbolise a kiss — *I love you xxxxxx* - but don't be taken in. It's a master of disguise and is just flirting with you. Don't trust it. It gives nothing away. X is the letter that marks the spot, the one that hides the booty on pirate maps, the letter they stick away in the files. X is harmful. If you don't believe me look on the back of a Domestos bottle. It's right there. It's official.

The sign says Welcome To The East Riding of Yorkshire, and who am I to argue. This is the flatland. The land with all the bumps and kinks ironed out, where everything is stretched and taut and the pylons look bigger. I pass a policeman playing with a speed gun on the hard shoulder. He's got that copper's grin and looks to be enjoying himself. In the distance I can see Goole docks and the cranes being all, er, crane-ish. Then, just before Junction 37, I drive up a slope that makes me feel like I'm on the Big Dipper and, matter-of-factly, I cross the Ouse.

It's a bit of a moment.

Symbolically this is where the 62 should finish. Rivers are natural boundary markers and the Ouse is where the mountain motorway should put its feet up and call it a day. But no, the 62 has to have its own way and just keeps on right on going.

Sod yer, it says.

The last bit of the 62 is orange. Really. The tarmac must have been bored being tarmac and fancied a change. It's not a bright orange but orange enough to be called orange. It suits it. I've never heard of an orange motorway before. I've heard of blue highways and yellow brick roads but an orange motorway is a new one to me.

The 62 finally just faded and fizzled out. I knew that because a road sign told me. Without turning off or switching direction I was suddenly driving on something called the A62, a two lane, everyday, no-big-deal kind of affair. I passed a Travel Lodge, a Little Chef and a petrol station and that was it. It was all over. The 62 was no more.

Coming back on the other side was like watching the same film on rewind. It was like going into a room full of mirrors and catching a quick glimpse of the back of your head. It was familiar yet totally strange at the same time.

I remember a policeman once telling me that there was no such thing as a fast lane on a motorway.

So, I asked him, by the same token, does that mean there's no slow lane then?

He just looked at me with a don't-push-it-sonny face. Slow lane or not that was the one I hugged all the way back from the Ouse to the Calder. In front of me was a battered old van. It was the colour of cold custard and had Mr Rainbow Ice Cream written across the back. He wasn't in a rush. Everybody went past us but what did I care? The 62 had taken me somewhere and now it was time to go somewhere else. I followed Mr Rainbow home.

Drive back from Leeds, turn off the 62 at Junction 25 and you'll see a caravan in a lay-by. Don't think Look-at-me-I've-got-a-chemical-toilet, a swanky double-bed and a nifty gas hob kind of caravan. Think the gaffer's office on an iffy building site. Think *Carry on Camping*. It's *that* kind of caravan. Four piles of housebricks keep it off the floor. You'd have to pay the scrappers to take it away. On the side in big green letters are the words *Le Fleur*.

That's class.

I remember once driving back from Leeds. Just a couple of days previous we'd found out that Jackie was pregnant with our first baby.

I pulled off the 62 and crossed Huddersfield Road to *Le Fleur*. I bought the biggest, silliest bunch of flowers they had. I don't know what kind they were. Uncle Fred would have told me. It was dark and cold. I could smell the bouquet. It smelt like the sun and made me feel warmer. I could see the artics on the motorway, those big 12-wheeler Scanias, Volvos and DAFs: *Norbert Dentressangle, Geest, Eddie Stobart.* They looked like they owned the road, 44-tons of testosterone, hugging the bumper of the car in front and itching to overtake. I could hear a noise that sounded like the sea. I heard a horn - *It's Grim Up North*. I thought about being a dad, a real dad. Blimey, I thought, now what? I looked at the motorway, that bloody road.

It still made me feel like a man.

Pocket Size

Rabbit : A Playlet

Outside the Olde Hatte. Early evening. Two kids, about the same age as Bart Simpson, are sitting on a rabbit hutch in the middle of the road. There is a third younger boy shoehorned inside the hutch. A man (me) approaches.

1st Boy :   Hey, do you wanna buy a rabbit hutch?

Man   :   Eh?

1st Boy :   *(aggressively)* This rabbit hutch. You buying it?

(Man shakes his head)

2nd Boy :   Why?

Man   :   I haven't got a rabbit.

2nd Boy :   Why?

(Man shrugs. Third boy wrestles himself out of the hutch)

1st Boy :   Go on. A tenner.

Man   :   Thanks, but no.

1st Boy :   S'good un. A Fiver.

Man   :   *(firmly)* I have no rabbit.

(Man walks away)

3rd Boy :   Bastard.

(Wrestles himself back into hutch)

Curtain

Looking for Bradley

I once knew this bloke who jacked in his job, scribbled a note for his wife and hopped aboard the first plane to India. When I asked him why he did it, he went all strange and mystical and mumbled something about wanting to find himself. Good luck to him. Personally, I don't have any problem finding myself. I wake up in a morning and hey presto, there I am, but I know what he means. Finding your self though, your real self, is easier said than done. Just which self are you looking for? The self that goes out with your mates on a Friday night or the one that watches rain drops dribbling down the window? People change all the time, everyone is someone else. You'll search and search and when you're convinced that you've found your true self, you'll find that that self is already out-of-date and you've become a nice, shiny new self. It's a bit of a poser.

For me, it starts with a name.

Some people, those who know what's what, call Yorkshire the Broad Acres. Other people, the kind that eat fig rolls and wear zip-up cardies with suede fronts, call it God's Own County. Let's leave them to it: Broad Acres is the name I'm interested in.

Talking of names, mine, Craig, comes from crag or rocky place and Bradley derives from broad lee, meaning big field or, wait for it, broad acres.

Broad Acres.

Well there you go, I couldn't have been born anywhere else.

I wanted my name to take me somewhere, to tell me things I didn't know about myself. I put the Crombie on and let my name tell its own story.

And this is it.

The Wrestler

Ladies and gentlemen, in the blue corner, weighing in at 220 pounds, please make some noise for the Halifax Hurricane himself, Mister Rocky Bigfield.
That's me in another life. Rocky Bigfield. It has a ring to it. Sounds like a pug-faced nightclub owner in a B-movie or an American wrestler.

The Butcher

So there you are. You're watching *YORKSHIRE – The Musical.* You're having a cracking time, a real beano. The songs are good, the cast is together, and the seats are comfy. York, Harrogate, Ripon, Leeds and all the rest of the A-Team are centre stage lovey-doveying in the limelight and milking the applause. Meanwhile, lurking backstage, Keighley is chewing its nails and stubbing a Regal King Size out on a No Smoking sign. Maybe one day it will get a big break but, for the moment, Keighley has to be content with a walk-on part.
On the road into Keighley from Halifax there used to be a butcher's shop. As butcher's shops go it was nothing special but it always caught my eye. Above the window, full of happy joints of beef and sad chicken legs, was the sign *CRAIG BRADLEY, BUTCHER.* I'd never seen my name that big before. I haven't seen it that big since. The first time I saw it, it caught me off guard, kind of rattled me a bit. That's my name, I thought, *my name*, what's going on here? I felt like people were looking at me, expecting me to do something.
Hey you with the big name, what's so special about you?
I'd stand outside the shop and look through the window. I wanted to see what this new version of Craig Bradley looked like. I wanted to hear him talk and laugh, to see if he sounded like me. I wanted to go in and buy a porkpie off myself.
Porkpie please Craig.
70 pence Craig.

There you go Craig.

Cheers Craig.

Cheers Craig.

It never happened. The last time I walked past I'd boarded the windows up and done a runner. God knows where I am now.

The Book

In the corner of the front room at home was a dusty old bookcase full of dusty old books. There was a complete set of Harmsworth Universal Encyclopaedias. These weighed a ton and belonged to the Granddad I never met. They were full of diagrams, maps and blurry black and white pictures of old admirals in silly hats. The old yellowy pages made a good crispy crinkly sound when you turned them over. I'd spend hours doing that. I'd lick my thumb and go for it. Forget the words I was happy just turning the pages over and over. They sounded like little thunderstorms.

Next to the Encyclopaedias was a red book called *The Complete Self Educator*. It had seen better days. It was tatty and torn with pages missing but it had chapters on everything. They had great names like *Physics - The Key to the Universe* and *Chemistry - The Secret of What Things Are*. *The Complete Self Educator* didn't have an author's name on the front. No-one knew who wrote it. Maybe it wrote itself. It was a magical book, full of keys and secrets. If you read it you'd be able to unlock things and know things that nobody else knew. Nobody in the world.

Another book I remember was *Bradley of the Fifth* written by someone called M Ireland. I don't know what the M stands for. Could be Malcolm, could be Montague, could be Mavis. Who knows? On the cover some posh kids in blue blazers were holding up a trophy and throwing their schoolcaps in the air. It was all a bit jolly hockeysticks for me, a bit la-de-dah. I never wore a school cap or a blazer. These were kids from a different age than me, a different world. They spoke another language. They called each other *chaps* and said things like *gosh, my word* and *frightfully queer*.

I didn't get it.

Bradley of the Fifth had one good thing going for it though, one thing that made up for all the *goshes* and *my words*. On the back of the first page was an inscription written in fountain pen. It was all flowing lines and fancy loops, more like drawing than writing. It said: *To Keith with love, from Mother Xmas 1942.* I liked that, it turned the book into a real living and breathing piece of history but, at the same time, it made me more cheesed off with the kids on the cover. There they were, with a war going on all around them and all these chaps can do is stand there in little blue blazers, throwing their caps in the air and going *Gosh, that's frightfully queer.*

Somebody should have given them the hard word.

The Tallest Man in England

I'm drinking hot coffee in a cold café and I'm talking to Bob. The café is part of the Londesborough Arms Hotel in Market Weighton, and Bob is giving me the once over.

So who you looking for again? he says.

Bradley, I said, I'm looking for Bradley.

He smiled.

Ah well then, come here.

Bob got up and took me to the Bradley Room. He pointed to a picture on the wall.

That's your man, he said.

I looked. Bob was right.

It was.

William Bradley, 1792-1820, was big, in fact he was bigger than big. Six feet six is big, six feet eight is bigger and six feet ten is getting silly. Bradley came in at seven feet nine - *seven feet nine* - all 27 stones of him. He fe-fi-fo-fummed his way around town on 15-inch feet and waved to people with hands big as wheelie-bin lids. The word is, Bradley was so tall he had to stand on a chair to put his hat on. In his day he was the tallest man in Yorkshire, in England and probably everywhere else. Forget the brick outhouse, Bradley was the brick outhouse with three downstairs rooms, a converted loft and a granny flat. Bradley was as big as they come. He was, in short, a giant.

There is a picture of the man himself on the wall of the Bradley Room. He's decked out in the gear of his time: frock coat – no Crombie for Billyboy - breeches, stockings and buckled shoes. He looks like a cross between a highwayman on his night off and the biggest, ugliest Prince Charming you've ever seen.

It was a Kodak moment. I'd have liked someone to take a snap of me looking at Bradley. I could have constructed my own little slice of eternity, a bit like holding one mirror up to another one. I could create a Bradley looking at Bradley who's looking at Bradley looking at Bradley kind of thing, and all this happening in the Bradley Room no less.

We could go on forever.

Bradley worked on the fairs as a freak. Had his own show, his own tent, the lot.

It was Bob talking.

Like the Bearded Lady, I said.

Bob nodded.

Yeah, he said, or the Elephant Man.

Bob gave me the old once over again.

You related? he said.

I studied Bradley's picture. I was looking for triggers, clues, Dad's chin, my nose, anything. I drew a blank.

Not that I know of, I said.

Bob sat in Bradley's seat that was underneath his picture. He looked like a kid in his dad's chair.

He liked a drop of the hard stuff and drank himself into an early grave, he said, they buried him next door in All Saints Church, just behind Going Places, the travel agents. Half the town had to carry his coffin.

I wouldn't mind a look at his grave, I said, must stand out a bit.

Bob shook his head.

Look all you like you won't find him here.

How d'you mean?

They kept digging him up, poor bugger, so they moved him.

Where to?

Bob shrugged.

Search me, he said.

I had another look at Bradley.

So, I said, he was a freak who drank too much eh? Maybe we are related.

Bob got out of the chair.

Maybe, he said.

All Saints Church was impressive. Not because it looked like a church should look, but the clock in the tower actually worked. It was half past two and still ticking. I walked around the graveyard. The names on the gravestones were good old salt-of-the-earth English ones: Crabtree, Pottage, Whittaker, Penrose and Ramsdale. There was a John Bradley but no William. It looked like Bob was right again. It started to rain. It was that soft rain which doesn't so much hit you as pat you on the head. It should always rain in graveyards, the two go together. Walk through a sunny graveyard and the people underneath you feel just that little bit more dead than they were before. The rain seems to perk them up a bit somehow, give them a bit of life back. I came to Market Weighton to look for Bradley. I'd found him and lost him again. I had one last look around, gave it up as bad job and made my way back to the Londesborough Arms.

A Man Called Truth

You'll find him in Brighouse cemetery.

Go through the main-gate by the Lodge, walk up the path, go under the archway by the boarded up chapel, past the leaky tap and the skip full of old wreathes and dead flowers and he's up there on the right. You can't miss him. Among the Johns and Alberts, Roberts and Harrys, his name stands out. Truth Berry. Go and look. No need to hurry, he isn't going anywhere.

For five hundred days I was a gravedigger. Do that job and it changes the way you look at a graveyard. Everyone else sees peace and eternal rest, I see backache and blisters. In the summer the job was a doddle, money for old rope. All you had to do was show up. In the winter though, you'd earn every penny, and then some. Snow, rain, freezing fog, whatever, you'd be out there. Graves don't dig themselves. During a cold snap the grass would stiffen with frost. When you nicked it with the halfmoon it lifted like Astroturf. Your fingers would go red then blue then red again. You'd dig just to get warm, happy away, keen to get in tune with the muck, the stones and the clay. Then there was the PCR, the Post-Christmas Rush. People would hold on for the turkey and sherry trifle then keel over after the Queen's speech. We couldn't dig graves fast enough. We'd get through two or three a day. I lived it and breathed it. I'd go to work and dig, come home and dig, then go to bed and dig some more. When I first started the quiet summers and busy winters threw me a bit. Nobody had told me that death was seasonal.

Being a gravedigger is good for you. Like being a baker, doctor or farmer it's one of the few real jobs left. Gravediggers have been around a long time. For as long as people have been dying, gravediggers have been spitting on their hands and getting on with it. If you think about it the guys who built the pyramids were just gravediggers with knobs on. OK they worked on a bigger scale, wore silly skirts and had cool names like Ozymandias but the end result was the same. And what about Hamlet? Who do you think dug up poor old Yorrick's skull? A technical resource manager? A recruitment consultant? A software engineer? I thinketh not.

Being a gravedigger is good for you on the outside and on the inside. On the outside you get fit, catch the sun and breathe as much fresh air as your lungs can hold. On the inside, the fact that you're doing something important makes you *feel* important. It hits you on a gut level. You get a buzz behind your belly and your soul starts smiling. But there's more to it than that, a lot more. For a start there's the technicalities of gravedigging and the architecture of dead people's resting places.

Not all dead people are six foot under. Forget that one for a start. Some are seven, some are five, some are four. It all depends on how many people want to use the grave. If Grandma wants to rest in peace with Granddad, then that's five feet. If little Jimmy wants to join mum and dad then it's six. If one more wants to go on top then you're looking at seven feet. Some are more, some are less. Some are bricked, some are earthen. No two are the same. People are different, even when they're dead.

Sometimes you have to re-open graves. Not in a Burke and Hare kind of way, but to make room for somebody else. These re-openers can be a bit on the tricky side. First you have to move the headstone. Slowly. If you crack it you'll be working for nothing for months. Then you take away the kerbs and urns, the vases and wreaths, the teddy bears and angels, the wind-chimes and birthday cards, flowerpots and photographs and then, and only then, you start digging. The ground has already been dug once so it's easy going. After a while you start to get near the coffin. You can tell that you're getting near because the sound of the soil changes and the shovel starts to sing a hollow, fat song. You soon learn the words. Then you tidy up and jump out double quick before the old lid gives way. It happens, especially when it's wet, heavy weather. Your boots can go right through the coffin lid and end up in the ribcage.

Squelch.

When that happens you just have to un-squelch yourself and say sorry. They don't seem to mind.

Graveyards aren't scary, or creepy or ghoulish. They're just full of people who once were and now are not. In all the time I worked in graveyards, all the graves I dug and the coffins I buried I never once got the jitters.

Well, maybe just the once.

It was my first re-opener. I got down to the box OK and was ready to jump out when the side of the box gave way. I fell back into the hole. I put my hands out to push myself up and grabbed something smooth, cold and round. I didn't have to look to know what it was. I had a skull in my hand. Not a normal everyday kind of skull. I could have dealt with that, this one was smiling at me. *Actually smiling.* I'm not making this up. It had a full set of teeth and was using them to flash me a big cheesy grin. Not only that but it was laughing. Not out loud like it would in a Stephen King book but inside my head. I could hear it crystal clear. It wasn't a spooky, eerie laugh but a jolly Uncle Jim kind of laugh. When that skull laughed at me I wanted to share the moment. I really did. I wanted to get in on the joke and laugh back. But I didn't. I couldn't. It's hard to laugh when you're in an open grave and you come face-to-face with the owner. You get the sweats and your mouth dries up. That day I was beaten, fair and square. I was outsmarted and outfoxed, by a dead man.

Uncle Jim is buried in a family plot that his dad Peter Bradley won in a game of poker. Stand at the graveside and you'll hear the dull hum of Keighley Road. On a weekday you can smell it, petrol fumes and bad eggs. Across the road from the graveyard used to be a pub called the Sportsman. It's not there anymore, it's been turned into luxury flats and I'm glad about that. Uncle Jim being buried opposite a pub called the Sportsman never made sense. Sport wasn't what he was about. He should have been resting in peace opposite a pub called the Dogbreeders Arms or the Spanner and Screw or something. That would have been more like it.

The grave itself is impressive. It must have been a serious game of poker. The monument is over seven feet high. There are names chiselled all over it and there's room for plenty more. At the funeral Dad told me that Jim wouldn't mind if I wanted to join him one day. The thought of it shook me up. I looked at Dad and then looked at him some more. It's not every day that your Dad turns into the Ghost of Christmas to Come.

My parents were geniuses. Not at rocket science or anything you can get out of a book, that's too easy. They were geniuses at being themselves, at being Mum and Dad. You try being a genius at being yourself, it's harder than you think. Every summer, when the long school holidays rolled around, Mum and Dad had to come up with something to occupy four kids. What did they do? Listen closely here because this is the genius bit. They took us to Bolton Abbey. Of course they did. Where else? There was nothing at Bolton Abbey, a load of nothing. Or at least there wasn't then. Nowadays there's a car park, souvenir shops, a café that charges you two quid for a pork pie, but waybackwhen, Bolton Abbey was a field, a river and a ruin. It wasn't Disneyland. It wasn't Alton Towers. It wasn't even Blackpool, but I loved it. I thought it was the best place on the planet, a big part of me still does. I'd slap on my Speedos and plunge straight into the Wharfe. Then, because the water was glacial, I'd plunge straight back out again. The Wharfe did things to you. It made you shiver and shake. It made you lose control of your teeth and made your jaw go funny. It stopped your lungs working properly. It made bits of you go numb and shrivel up. Thirty years later and I can still feel it. Bits of me are still numb and shrivelled up. That's the Wharfe for you. And I loved it.

After the river came the ruin or the Priory to use its Sunday name. It always caught the eye. It was as much a part of the landscape as the trees and the hills around it and looked as old as the river itself. I always thought that it looked asleep and that one day it will yawn and stretch itself awake. Then I used to get scared and stopped thinking about it.

The Priory might be a ruin but it never looked like it was falling down. Not to me. It looked like it was built that way. It might have a five o'clock shadow and a bad case of bedhead but that shabbiness suits it. You sense that it's not trying to impress, that it's at ease with itself. There's a lesson in there somewhere if you look hard enough.

The Priory was a top place for exploring. I used to imagine I was one of those posh kids in the *Famous Five* books I got for Christmas. I'd drink lashings and lashings of ginger beer, even though I didn't have a clue what a lashing was, and then I'd swan around being clever and solving mysteries. I'd run under the big arches and lob pebbles through the windowless windows. I'd walk through the graveyard looking at the names on headstones. I'd sit down and imagine what kind of people those names belonged to. Come to think of it, I was a bit of a weirdo.

One gravestone though, got me thinking. On it was the name Elijah Moon: Died 1914 aged 80. I liked the name, the sound of it and the pictures it painted. I never met Elijah but we were mates. Best mates. We hung about together in my head. I promised him that if I ever got famous I'd use his name somewhere. I thought if I played cricket for Yorkshire I'd call myself Elijah Moon - *And Elijah Moon majestically hits yet another sensational six and Yorkshire triumph again.* I thought if I ever made it as a rock star I'd use it as the name of my band. *Elijah Moon: Live at Wembley Stadium. ALL TICKETS SOLD OUT.* But I never did hit that six or play Wembley so Elijah was left on his lonesome.

Or at least he was until 25 years later. I was walking past the graveyard when I remembered Elijah. I couldn't remember his last name but I knew it was cosmic and had something to do with the stars. I knew where he was and I checked him out. Elijah Moon. He'd been stuck in my head in the file marked *Slightly Scary Memories* for years. I still liked the name, it still stood out. I still felt a bond with someone who'd died 50 years before I was born. Crazy? Probably. It wasn't Elijah's fault. I was the one making the connection. It was all down to me. I got my two quid pork pie out and sat down to think things through. I could find out more about Elijah. I could ask around and cobble some facts together. But why bother? This isn't about Elijah. It's about being a kid and the having the memories that go with it. The Elijah I have in my head, the one I hung about with years ago, has nothing to do with the real blood and guts version; the Elijah that lived and breathed, loved and laughed. My Elijah is just a name that I turned into a memory. And what are names anyway? They're only made of letters and letters make words and words are hot air and so on. It all gets a bit fuzzy after that. When I finished my pie though, two things were clear: one; it wasn't worth two quid and two; I still am a weirdo.

Which brings me back to where I started: A Man called Truth. Sounds like a rainy Sunday afternoon western on BBC2. Imagine the young Henry Fonda, rolling into town. I can see him now - *I done hear tell that some folks round these parts have been caterwauling me behind my back, well my name is Truth and that's what I aim to find. Yessir.*

There are no lies in a graveyard. No grey areas. The dead are dead and that's that. I should know, I've buried enough. Some graves though stay with you, Elijah Moon and Truth Berry are names I won't forget.

Truth.

Try the word.

Go on. Whisper it. Shout it.

TRUTH.

No matter how you say it you've got to admit one thing: it's the perfect name for a dead man.

Pocket Size

Showtime on the 42

Noddy Holder is sitting opposite me on the number 42. Not the *actual* Noddy Holder but close enough to deserve the name. His head wobbled and his eyes glazed. He looked at himself in the bus window, smiled a half smile and winked. He looked at me. In fact he looked right through me.

Unblinking.

Lizardlike.

He leaned forward and opened a mouth that was too big for his face.

You are so beautiful to me.

He was loud, foghorn loud. Everybody on the bus turned my way. I scratched a nose that wasn't itching and cleared a throat that didn't need clearing. Then Noddy went all Joe Cocker on me again.

You are so beautiful to me. Can't you see?

Show over, he sat back and smiled. Then he started snoring, with his eyes open.

Next stop two old blokes got on and made a beeline straight for me. They were apple-cheeked and too happy to be sober. One wore a trilby, the other was hatless.

Hey lad, the Trilby said, I'll be 85 tomorrow.

Hatless interrupted before I had the chance to butt in.

Who wants to be eighty bloody five?

The Trilby looked at me and slapped my thigh.

The fella who's eighty bloody four, he said.

Noddy just winked at himself again.

House Music

When you're the youngest you don't make your own mistakes, you just remake someone else's. Your shoes, your shirts, your trousers, the coat on your back, they all come to you second-hand. And it's not just clothes. It's the same with thoughts, ideas, words – you only say bloody because you heard Dad say it when he got a shock fixing the electric doorbell – DING BLOODY DONG – and it's the same with music, especially the music.

It's all my big brother's fault.

The first ever LP I bought was The Muppets double album. I liked it. I played it a lot. The songs still go round in my head. *Lydia the Tattooed Lady, Hey Mister Bassman, you've got that certain something,* when Kermit's nephew Robin sang *Halfway Down the Stairs,* I was sat right there next to him. I knew where he was coming from – *It's not at the bottom, it's not at the top, but this is the stair where I always stop.* Oh yes. I hear you Robin, I hear you. But Mark, my big brother, didn't hear him. He'd had enough and decided I needed help, big help, and I needed it right now. Exit Kermit and co and enter Black Sabbath.

Life was never the same again.

When I was a kid I was scared of the dark, really scared. It was full of everything and nothing and frightened every inch of me. My feet got scared, my ears, my fingers, you name it, every piece of me quaked. Every creak on the stairs was a loony with an axe coming to chop me into a million pieces. I'd curl up into a tight ball on the top-bunk and hold my breath. I could hold my breath forever, even longer if I had to. I'd listen to my blood rushing and hear my heart pumping.

Thumpthump.

Thumpthump.

It was like being in one of those scary films with Vincent Price. You know something bad is going to happen when you hear a heartbeat. It's a nailed on, dead cert.

Thumpthump.

Thumpthump.

Oh yes, the loony with the axe was getting closer and closer.

I liked to hear Dad coughing in the next room. He didn't do it a lot, just now and again, to clear his throat. I suppose it made a change from snoring all night. Dad's coughs made me feel safe, like I wasn't alone. It was even better when he got up to pee: suddenly the world was a cosy, warm place. Dad would pee straight into the middle of the bowl. No messing. It was loud and splashy and suddenly the dark didn't seem as dark anymore. Dad's pee made the night lighter and the loony go away. Then he'd go back to bed, cough a bit and start snoring again. And then it would get darker and darker and scarier and scarier and the stairs would get creakier and creakier - *the loony was on his way again.* It was there and then, in the middle of the darkest, scariest, creakiest night in the entire history of the entire world that Mark decided to play some music by a band who sang songs about war and witches and devils.

Just what I needed.

The thing about big brothers is that they stay big. Even if you dare to be so stupid as to actually grow half an inch taller than your big brother it won't make a difference. He is the big one and you are the little one. Get used to it. That's how the big brother/little brother thing works.

Sabbath scared me to death. The leap from Kermit to Ozzy was too big and I just wasn't ready for them. Mark slept like a baby listening to *War Pigs, Fairies Wear Boots* and *Iron Man.* Not me. How could you sleep through all that? Listening to Sabbath was like having the Devil sat on the end of your bed. I could smell him. I could feel him. I could see him, if I shut my eyes and looked hard enough. I wanted Dad to cough or pee.

Pleeeeeeease.

A really long cough would have done the job or a big, bladder-busting pee. That's all I wanted to hear. I didn't get it. I wasn't halfway down the stairs anymore. Oh no. Things had moved on. I was on my own now. I was trapped in a pitch black bedroom with the Prince of Darkness himself.

Fast forward ten years and I'm in the Queen's Hall in Leeds. Sabbath are on stage. Queen's Hall was a cross between an airport hanger and a butcher's fridge. It was full of puddles and had these big, ugly concrete pillars that held the roof up. If you got stuck behind one of those you didn't see anything except, well, a big, ugly concrete pillar that held the roof up. Queen's Hall is heaving with sweaty bodies and the meatheads are giving it the biglicks down the front. It's hot, dark and louder than the word loud itself. I'm listening to Sabbath but I'm not really there at all. I'm years away back in Halifax. I'm waiting for the loony to come up the stairs and I'm wishing Dad would go for a pee. I'm curled up in a tight ball and holding my breath in the top-bunk.

I was happy being *Halfway Down The Stairs* but it wasn't enough. Over the years I've spent thousands on singles, albums, tapes, CDs, videos, tickets, bootlegs, t-shirts, sweatshirts, posters and concert programmes. I've queued up for hours and hours in the rain. I've seen bands that made my ears ring for days and days. I'm going to go deaf when I'm older, I just know it. I'll go around shouting at people and scaring small children. I'm going to turn into Reg Sykes. I've had a life-long love affair with music that is years and years out of date. I feel like some kind of dinosaur when I talk about it. Young people look at me and go *Aw bless*. But it still gets me, that same music that once scared me to death, it still hits the spot. I was happy being *Halfway Down The Stairs* but it wasn't enough and all of it, every bit, is my big brother's fault.

And I'm still half an inch taller.

Our house was like a big jukebox. Every room had its own sound, its own rhythm.

Mum was into Barry Manilow and Tom Jones. She'd play their records every Sunday morning on the Philips record player in the front room. Mum liked Barry because he was a nice looking kind of boy who sang cute songs like *Can't Smile Without You* and *Mandy*. Mum liked Tom because he wasn't a boy at all but a real macho man with a big voice and tight trousers. I couldn't blame her. When I saw Tom on telly I fancied him myself.

Mum used to play Tom at the weekend when she was cleaning the house. She'd turn him up loud. I hear *It's Not Unusual* now and I think of Sunday mornings and the hoover banging against the bedroom door.

Elvis belonged to Dad. He talked about him like he knew him. It was Elvis this and Elvis that. He did the same with Frank Sinatra and Louis Armstrong. For years I thought that Elvis, Frank and Louis were builders in Halifax who did a bit of singing in the clubs at the weekends. If I'd have come home and seen Dad sat at the table drinking tea with The King, Old Blue Eyes and Satchmo I wouldn't have batted an eyelid. I'd have just said hello and put the kettle on.

One lump or two Mr Presley?

I have two older sisters which means that when I was growing up I had two stand-in mums on the subs bench. When the real Mum was busy one of my sisters would take over and start saying things like *wash your face, put your coat on* and *eat your dinner*. Y'know, Mum's stuff.

My sisters were into David Cassidy, Donny Osmond and David Essex. I'd hear their songs through the wall - *Daydreamer, Puppy Love, Hold Me Close*. I saw the posters pinned all over their bedroom wall. David Cassidy looked like a girl and Donny Osmond smiled too much. I bet he'd never worn his big brother's shirts. I hated him. But David Essex was different. I liked him. I liked his collarless shirts, his waistcoats and, most of all, I liked his name.

David Essex.

Imagine being called after a whole county. I'd never been to Essex but I found it on the map. It was where London fans out a bit and goes up into Suffolk. Colchester was in Essex and I knew that anywhere that ends in Chester used to be a roman fort, so it sounded pretty good to me. I thought about being a popstar. I reckoned it would be a good job. You got to wear cool shirts with no collars and dance around in your Granddad's waistcoat. I was going to go on *Top of the Pops.* I'd get introduced by Jimmy Saville or DLT.

And next is the man all you girls have been waiting for.

I was going to have my own fan club and a wall full of gold discs.

The man of the moment.

I was going to have a big hit that stayed at number one for weeks and weeks and weeks.

Let's hear it for Craig Yorkshire.

Then everyone would scream and all the girls would go red and start fainting.

But they never did.

In 75 Al Wilson released a single called *The Snake.* Ask me about Al Wilson and you'll draw a blank. Zilch. I don't know if he's fighting fit or has breathed his last. I don't know if he's black or white, rich or poor. I don't know if he tucks his shirt into his trousers, prefers boxers to briefs or whisky to wine. He might be the kind of bloke who thinks he's funny and goes round saying things like – *Not three bad* - or - *Hey look who it isn't.* He might be the one who writes I WISH THE WIFE WAS THIS MUCKY on the back of dirty transit vans. I don't know. Ask me about *The Snake* though and it's a different story.

Oh yes.

Dad had a Cortina Mk1. Midnight-blue. DLK 737C. I remember that because Auntie Dulce said DLK stood for Dear Loving Keith. Keith is Dad by the way. Dad was tickled pink with the Cortina because it had a heated rear window. He'd switch this fancy new gizmo on and off willy-nilly in the middle of summer – *For the bloody ell of it* – then start singing *What a Wonderful World* at full blast.

Me and Louis Armstrong go back a long way.

The first time I heard Louis sing I thought the record player was on the blink or something. Nobody sings like that, he sounded like smoky treacle. Mum used to say that if Yorkshire had a voice it would sound like Louis. Yeah it would, but with a Barnsley accent. Dad did a decent impression. It made his face go red and he couldn't do it for a long time but close your eyes and Mr Smoky Treacle himself was sat right next to you. *What a Wonderful World* was Louis's last big hit and he sings it like he knew it.

I see trees of green, red roses too.
I watch 'em bloom, for me and you.

It might be cheesy, but it's the best cheese you can get.

And I think to myself, what a wonderful world.

Pure Wensleydale.

The Cortina looked like the Batmobile. It had the same kind of backlights, a kind of magical crime-fighting circle full of triangles. It had a heated rear, four doors, five gears and enough room for six of us. What it didn't have was a radio.

Enter Al Wilson.

Some well-meaning fool bought my well-meaning sister Kay a well-meaning tape-recorder for Christmas. It was weird listening to yourself talk back to you. I sounded like a pig farmer who'd had a stroke. Kay used to tape the Top 40 Chart Show on Sunday nights. She'd shush us all and hold the mike up to the radio. It worked. Now and again you'd get some background noise. You'd be grooving out to *Whispering Grass* by Windsor Davies and Don Estelle and someone would sneeze or fart. Kay would give us daggers. I thought it made the song better, kind of personalised it. Anyway Al released his *Snake,* Kay bought it, taped it and played it in the Batmobile over and over.

And over again.

Take me in oh tender woman
Take me in for heaven's sake
Take me in oh tender woman
Sssssssighed the snake.

We Batmobiled all over our world: Bolton Abbey, Shipley Glen, Skipton, Scarborough, Filey, you name it. And there was Al singing his heart out like a trooper. Al was soul, northern soul and even now I can't drive through Bridlington without sighing like Al's snake.

Sssssssssss.

Eventually the Batmobile had enough and the sub-frame snapped. The tape-recorder got the elbow to make way for a record-player, but what about poor old Al? I like to think that he's out there somewhere singing his little love songs about reptiles with cylindrical bodies, cold blood and no eyelids.

Bless his cottons.

Different places have different sounds. The city needs something sparkly, something with a bit of fizz. Drive through Leeds, Sheffield, Hull, Bradford and you need music that can stand up on its own two legs and won't embarrass itself in good company. Music that looks people in the eye and doesn't get cut up in traffic. Jimi Hendrix always works for me, The Beatles, Otis Redding, Sinatra when he was swinging, the Stones on a good day, that kind of stuff. It's slick but not too polished, confident but not too big for its boots, big music for the big city.

The Dales though have a different sound. Out there you need songs that can handle the big spaces, tunes that won't blow away on the breeze. Out there you need the blues. Nothing too rootsy: BB King, Johnny Winter, early Zeppelin, take your pick. When that music locks into the landscape everything clicks into place. It's like being in the band that are playing the soundtrack to your life.

True story. I was driving across Ilkley Moor. It was pouring down, when suddenly it cleared up and the rain stopped. It was like a big hand somewhere had turned off the tap. The sun squinted out from behind the clouds and suddenly the day was full of rainbows. Big, beautiful, drunken rainbows. There they were, in glorious technicolour. I pulled up by the Cow and Calf Rocks to look for the pot of gold. I sat there just staring at the colours. They were splashed across the sky and I wanted to take them all in. I counted them – *Richard Of York Gave Battle In Vain* – they were psychedelic. I clicked the radio on and found a station. It was a big moment and I needed a big song, a song as big as everything. This is what I got:

Take me in oh tender woman
Take me in for heaven's sake.

Wait a minute. What's he doing on the radio? He's never on the radio.

Take me in oh tender woman.

But he was.

It was Al. He was still doing it, still ssssighing like a snake. It was perfect, like meeting an old friend. The car was full of northern soul and no-one knew about it except Al, the rainbows and me. It was our secret. The song finished and I clicked the radio off. It was over. Nothing could top that.

Balls, Battles and Brown Envelopes

Balls

Boxing Day. Halifax Town v Scarborough. I support Halifax for one reason, I was born there. I also support Scarborough. Why not? I like the place. I like the castle, the beach and the cut of its jib. So I have a problem, a football pitch sized problem.

Except I don't.

I want Town to win. Course I do. But not just to win.

Oh no no no.

Merely winning isn't enough, not by a long-chalk. I want them to take Boro apart. I want them to walk all over them in the first half and then rub their noses in it in the second. I want them to heartlessly grind Boro into the grey Halifax dust. And then grind some more. I want to see grown men weeping and crying for their mothers.

And let me tell you why.

Being born in a place triggers a connection that starts before you arrive and carries on after you kick the bucket. It's a connection that lasts longer than a lifetime. Your home town is the place where you roll into being and your own history starts. It provides you with the ancestral cloth from which you are cut. Wherever your ship may sail your home town anchors you to a past you can never really leave. No matter how hard you try. Like it or lump it your birthplace is always with you. It's in the air you breathe and the words you speak. Sometimes it's your best friend. It slaps you on the back, flashes a smile and opens doors for you. Sometimes it's the biggest bastard in town. Sometimes it's so quiet you hardly notice it. You start to think it's had enough, that it's done a runner. Don't be fooled. It's there. All you can do is get used to it.

Football and me have never really got on. Not if I cross my heart and hope to die. I've tried. I've done my share of keepy-ups, hit enough balls against enough walls. I even made left back at primary school, but only because Mr Briers, the Maths-cum-English-cum-Science-cum-PE-cum-Everything teacher, wanted a big numb bugger at the back to deal with goal kicks and go up for corners. As big numb buggers go I was top of the list. I turned up, ran about a bit then went home rubbing my head. We must have been half decent because we got some kind of medal. It had a little silver bloke on it kicking a little silver ball. It wasn't a big deal, not to me. My best sporting achievement is winning the Tug o'War at the Halifax Schools Sports Day 1974. *That* was a big deal, getting a rope-burn that made your hands look like raw liver, now that *was* sport, my kind of sport. I even got a certificate signed by Mr Lewis the Headmaster. Mum was proud. It was the first certificate I ever got for anything. Football? You could keep it.

And it's not just football. The other ball games: cricket, golf, rugby, even snooker, I've tried them all at some point. In August 1977 we were in the Batmobile driving down to Cornwall for our holidays. England were playing Australia at Headingley and Geoff Boycott was slowly nudging toward his 100th hundred. It kept coming on the radio:

Boycott is on 33 not out.

Boycott is on 56.

Boycott is on 78.

Things got a bit nervous in the nineties. I bit my nails and drummed my fingers a lot. It seemed to take forever for Geoff to get to the magical number. But, finally, *finally:*

Boycott has done it, he has made his century.

I'd never met Geoff Boycott, never shook his hand or shared a word but when I heard that this Yorkshire-man, perhaps *the* Yorkshire-man, had made his 100th century at Headingley, against the Aussies, I felt I knew him. I really did. At that moment I felt that Geoff and me were the bestest mates in the whole wide world.

Then it all got a bit weird.

I used to watch Test Matches on telly and pretend I was playing. I'd crouch in a fielding position on the rug in the front room waiting for the batsman to send a thick edge my way, so I could dive like a hero and catch it. I really thought it could happen. I'd crouch there all day. I'd stop for drinks and have tea at the same time as the players. If I'd have had some white pants I'd have worn them. If rain stopped play I sat on the settee and looked at the sky. If there was bad light then I'd look at the sky again but do it in the dark. I wasn't just watching the cricket on the telly. This was the real thing. I was one of the team. *I was there.*

What a weirdo.

Golf came and went. On holiday Dad and me always checked out the Crazy Golf courses. Dad played for laughs and just liked hitting the ball up ramps, round corners and through little windmills but not me, oh no, I was dead serious. I was playing in the British Open. I'd line up putts, check my grip and turn into Jack Nicklaus. It didn't work and Dad beat me every time.

My rugby league career is a bit more complicated. I just didn't like the game. To me it was like one big muddy scrap that gave people an excuse to kick seven bells out of each other. I only got picked for my secondary school team because I was bigger than Robbo, the Games teacher. I had no choice. Robbo would write up his team sheet every Friday. Then, he'd light his pipe and read it out to us.

Ingham and Sutcliffe: props, Robbo would say, Cook and Bradley: second row.

But sir, I'd say.

Bradley, second row.

But sir.

Then Robbo would pull that face that only teachers can pull and point his pipe at me.

But nothing lad, he'd say, second row.

And that sealed it.

The first game I played I made a bad mistake: I scored a try. I can't remember much about it. I think I was running about, more to keep warm than anything else, when out of the blue I got the ball. I wasn't looking for it, it just appeared in my hands. I kept on going until people started slapping me on the back saying well done. Robbo was puffing away on his pipe and smiling at me from the touchline.

Played, he said.

Played, my arse, I should have told him where to stick his bloody pipe.

My snooker period was a low point. Dad picked up a second hand table that had a lead base and weighed a ton. It was so big we had to keep it in the garage. When we wanted a game we'd grunt and groan and carry it into the house and set it up in the dining room. You could put your back out. The cushions had lost their bounce and the balls were the wrong size for the pockets. It didn't really matter. I only played snooker because I wanted a cool nickname like Alex *Hurricane* Higgins. I experimented with a few: *The Storm* and *The Tornado* were just a couple I tried out but they didn't sound right. I finally settled for Craig *The Breeze* Bradley. That did the business. I even bought a cue from my mate. It came in its own case and you had to screw it together. I was a pro. Nobody would be able to beat me now. One day when Dad asked me if I fancied a game I had to laugh. Did he really want to play *The Breeze?* OK, I said, with a smug smirk, I'll take it easy with you. I never got the chance. Dad hammered me. He made the cue ball go where he wanted it to and potted the wrong sized balls in the wrong sized pockets. That was it. The table went back in the garage, the cue went back in the case and *The Breeze* called it a day.

My brother Mark liked football. Well, he did before the rugby bug bit him. Then he got hard and called football a game for puffs. In the early 70s Mark supported Leeds but so did everybody else. Even teams that played against Leeds supported Leeds. I remember watching the 1973 Cup Final. Leeds v Sunderland. I remember Dad shouting at the telly a lot. I remember getting a screwball from the ice cream van at half-time. I remember Leeds losing. I wasn't bothered. I'd got a screwball out of it.

At that time Dad worked for a firm called Grimston's Garages. The garages came in bits, like big Meccano kits, and Dad drove all over the place in his big yellow wagon putting them together. Grimston's had a showroom in Leeds opposite the Elland Road ground. Now and again Dad would pop into the local greasy spoon for a breakfast and see the Leeds team wolfing down their pre-training fry-ups. Builders and top notch footballers in the same café eating the same food from the same plates. Talk about times-a-changing. I'm no expert but I can't imagine Beckham polishing off a quick egg butty before practising his free-kicks. I only wish he would. Come on Golden Balls do it for me. And while you're at it your missus looks like she could use a bacon butty or two.

Dad's claim to fame is that he built Jackie Charlton's garage. Jackie had a posh house in a posh part of Leeds and fancied somewhere to park his posh car. He got on the blower to Grimston's and before he could say *Play to feet and keep it tight at the back*, Dad was on the case. Jackie was so chuffed with his new purchase he gave Dad a crate of Newcastle Brown as a thank you. It stood in the garage at home for weeks. Dad can't stand the stuff.

Do you really want me to tell you about the weather? Thought as much. Let's just say it was the kind of weather the Crombie was made for. I was glad to be wearing it. I'm at the Shay, sat in the Cowshed supping instant tomato soup from a polystyrene cup. At least I think it's tomato soup. It's either that or very red tea. In front of me is a bloke in a Santa Claus hat. His festive headgear doesn't match his un-festive face. I was going to say cheer up mate it might never happen, but one quick look at him told you it already had. Behind me is a bloke called Harry. Harry doesn't talk, he shouts. He wants us all to share in his wisdom. He's generous that way. He shouts things like:

Pathetic.

Useless.

Bloody rubbish.

And that's before the kick-off. I don't know what Harry looks like. I don't even know if Harry's called Harry. I don't need to. I've built up a perfect picture of him. He's pushing seventy. He wears a scruffy raincoat that Columbo wouldn't be seen dead in. He has bad teeth and a beard. He'll never buy a cuppa, not in a million years, but he's more than happy to give you a dirty look as you drink yours. Don't ask me how I know these things I just do. Every time I've been down the Shay I always get a Harry behind me. God knows where they spring from.

Maybe there's a nest of them somewhere. Every time there's a game on they crawl out from under their rock and sit behind me.

Shouting.

The ref blew for kick-off. Then he blew again. Then again. In fact he didn't stop blowing. I don't know why. Nobody knew why. A 50-50 ball? He'd blow. A shoulder charge? He'd blow. A dirty look? He'd blow. Stop, start, stop, start. It was like watching a football version of musical chairs. Harry wasn't impressed.

Flippin stupid bugger.

Give it a bloomin rest ref.

For God's sake, let em play soddin football will yer.

Harry only used Conference League swear words.

Scarborough looked handy enough. They had a big striker whose name was so long there was hardly room for it on the back of his shirt. There wasn't much in it for the first half-hour. Both teams were happy just to boot the ball into the wind and see where it ended up. The pundits call it Route One Football. Whatever it was, it was getting comments.

It's a good job this int on Sky.

You'd have been better stayin 'ome an watchin *The Wizard of Oz*.

Then on 35 minutes the game took a different turning.

It all got a bit hazy.

Somebody slid into a bone-splitting tackle. A leg-breaker, Harry called it. Somebody didn't like it and somebody threw a right hook. Somebody forgot to duck and somebody went down. Then before the ref could blow, everything kicked off and a cartoon fight broke out. It looked like Popeye going toe-to-toe with Bluto. All I could see were arms and legs. The ref blew until he went a funny colour then somebody else played prefect and broke it up. Lots of finger wagging and he-started-it gestures followed before the man in black got his red card out and sent four players off, two from each side. It gave the terraces something to talk about at half-time.

This could end up five-a-side.

They've mentioned it on *Five Live*. If two more from the same side get sent off then they'll have to postpone the game. It'll be the first time that's happened for 37 years.

Bloody ell, we might make history.

We'll get in the papers.

Aye, mebbe the nationals.

It was time for some more red tea.

When Teletext later called the game - *a fiery Yorkshire derby* - they weren't joking. The players seemed a little more focused in the second half. Focused is football lingo for looking like they wanted to rip each other's throats out. The big Boro player with the long name made some good runs and there were a few scrambles at both ends. Harry wasn't bothered. He was just happy shouting at the ref.

You dipstick.

Gerra flamin grip man.

Yer nowt but a blinkin little Hitler.

Blinkin, he actually said *blinkin*.

Then out of nothing Town scored. I knew they'd scored because all the home fans started singing - *You're Not at the Seaside Anymore* - to the Boro faithful. I heard some loudmouth chanting - *Come on Shaymen. Come on Shaymen.* I recognised the loudmouth's voice.

It was mine.

Something tribal was happening inside me, something beyond football. I was shouting at myself, at my own history and the history of those who came before me. I was on my feet, clapping and cheering. My team, my *home town* team were winning, really winning. Then the ref blew and Halifax had done it. We'd gone and bloody done it. It felt good. Better than good. Maybe I've been too harsh about football. Maybe we get on better than I thought. I didn't know the game could move me like this.

Football?

It's fan-*blinkin*-tastic.

Battles

What is it like to get punched full in the face by someone wearing a boxing glove? I'm asking a mate of mine who's done a bit in the ring.

Dunno, he says with a wink, never been hit.
I keep pushing.
Come on, I say.
He thinks for a while.
It's like an orgasm, he says.
An orgasm, I say, who've you been sleeping with?
No really it is, he says, he's getting serious. I get a real rush and I know, I just know, that I'm gonna kill whoever it is in front of me.
I nod.
Blimey.

I'm in Doncaster at the Dome. In my hand is a FIGHT SKOOL ticket. It's an evening of boxing and they've made it sound like a Slade B-side. I'm sat in the Ice Breaker Lounge having, well, an ice breaker I suppose. The bar is packed with men: big men, small men, fat men, thin men, ugly men and uglier men, there's no room in boxing for pretty boys. They're at the bar, sitting on chairs, leaning up against the wall and queuing up for the toilet. There is smoke on top of smoke and the banter is louder than the juke box. Everyone is talking a good fight. Some men look like they know what they are talking about and some men look like they don't know what day it is. Me, I just look like a bloke in a big coat. One bloke stood next to me is wearing the full works: dinner suit, cummerbund and dicky bow. He's got Brylcreamed hair and he's smoking a twenty quid cigar. I ask him how it's going. He looks at me, takes a drag and then crushes his cigar under his well polished brogue.

That's how it's going, he said and walked away.

I'm not sure but I think he growled at me.

I look around and take a sniff. There's no doubt about it. The whiff of testosterone is so strong you could chop it up with a cleaver and take it home in a butcher's bucket.

I make my way through to the ring and the doorman rubber-stamps PAID on the back of my hand. I like it. It looks like a prison tattoo. I'm looking around at the blue ring with the blue ropes and the Sky Sports logo when I hear a bell. Suddenly, it's Seconds Out, Round One.

First up is a Light-Heavyweight contest between Dean Cockburn and Gary Thompson. Cockburn is a local hero and calls himself the Donny Bomber. Thompson isn't a local hero and calls himself Thompson.

Fair enough.

The Donny Bomber is up for it and Thompson looks edgy. His eyes are darting all over the place and his body language is sending out mixed signals. Half of it's saying – *Come and have a go local boy, I'm not scared of you* – and the other half is saying – *Look, can't we just go for a pint and talk this over?* The crowd feel it and get behind their man.

C'MON DEANO.

C'MON DEANO.

C'MON DEANO.

Things are getting loud. Thompson licks his lips. He looks worried, he has every right to be. He wasn't just fighting Deano, he was in the ring with half of Doncaster.

Deano ran out on the bell and threw some big right-hands. He looked like a man who wanted to get the job done, a real barnburner of a fighter. To his credit Thompson rolled with the punches, used his feet and kept working on his jab. He had a lot of heart and wasn't going to roll over.

By the end of the first round the crowd had come up with some new lyrics.

USE THE BODYSHOTS.

OVER THE TOP.

DO HIM DEANO.

In the 4th Deano did him. He caught Thompson with a good left hook, followed it up with a few digs to the ribs and Thompson went down. He got to his feet and took a standing count until the ref decided that enough was enough and the Donny Bomber won with a Technical Knock Out. The crowd got what they wanted.

On my way to the toilet I met WBU World Light Welterweight champion, Ricky *The Hitman* Hatton. What do you do when you meet a world champion boxer on the way to the loo? Let me tell you what I did.

I shook Ricky's hand and called him mate.

Mate.

Hello mate, I said. It was like we grew up together.

It was the wrong word. Boxers aren't matey people, especially world champions. A boxer is not your cheeky-chappy window cleaner, always ready with a smile and a quick joke. He's not the landlord of your local or that bloke from Kwik-Fit who changes your exhaust and knocks you a fiver off for cash. *They're* mates, real mates. But boxers aren't like that. They live by their own rules and operate in a different world. Boxing is full of hard stares, mindgames and meaningful silences. It's a world full of men who get paid to hurt each other. I remember Joe Frazier once saying that boxing isn't about the fight, it's about you and the other guy. There's no room for mates.

Second on the bill are Lightweights Steffy Bull v Jimmy Beech. Bull is Central Area Champion and looks like a lot of people. He looks like a bass player in a punk band that never quite made it. He looks like one of those small time baddies that Bruce Willis has to beat up before he gets to Mr Big, and he looks like a squaddie from the 1940's. He's got that kind of face. He's also got spiky blonde hair, a six-pack stomach and his own fan club. When Bull climbed into the ring the tone of the crowd changed. It became higher pitched and I heard something that wasn't there before. I listened hard. Yep, there was no doubt about it.

Women.

I looked behind me and the whole row was full of screaming, giggling, red-faced women. I don't know where they came from. They must have been beamed up from somewhere. There were 15 or so of them, all popped up and ready to rumble. They looked like a Poundstretcher version of the Spice Girls. It was scary.

BULLY.

KNOCK HIM OUT.

KEEP HIM IN RANGE AND WORK HIM.

The Spice Girls knew what they were talking about.

Bull had a Muhammad Ali tattoo on his right shoulder. At least I think it was Ali, but from where I was sitting it could have been anybody from Gary Wilmot to Lenny Henry. Bull was impressive. He was aware of the crowd, worked the room and did a touch of showboating: a smile here, a wink there. It was just another day at the office.

In the 3rd Bull started to get on top. His punches were hitting home. Beech tried to hold on. The Spice Girls weren't impressed.

STOP TRYING TO SNOG HIM WILL YER.

When the bell went at the end of the fight there was only ever going to be one winner. Bull had done it.

Doncaster 2, Everywhere Else 0.

Things moved up a notch with the third fight. This was the first eight-rounder on the card. The intro music got louder and so did the shorts. *Magic* Matthew Hatton – my mate's brother - in camouflage shorts v Francis *The Rat* Jones wearing red shorts with white trim. I don't know why Jones calls himself the Rat. Maybe he's slippery and hard to fight. Maybe he'll turn on you if you get him in a corner. Or maybe the only way to beat him is to hit him really hard over the head with a shovel.

Whatever his reasons I suppose it's better than calling yourself *the Mouse*. That wouldn't scare anyone.

Even though neither fighter was from Doncaster the crowd were still getting behind them.

SHOW US SOME MAGIC.

C'MON ROLAND.

I was sat in the noisiest, booziest part of the crowd. And that's just me.

USE YOUR RIGHT.

JAB RAT.

Jab, I like that word.

Jab.

Jab.

Jab.

I had a thought: what about opening a gym for unemployed boxers and calling it the Jab Centre.

Maybe not.

I sat back and watched Magic and Rat go toe-to-toe. I let the fight take over. It had a rhythm and a swing all of its own. There was a lot of leather flying about and both fighters seemed to know what the other one was going to do. The only thing that spoilt it was the referee. While football refs at least try to look the part, boxing refs just look like drunken uncles at weddings. It's the dicky bow that does it. They go all red-faced and sweaty and look like they've been raving all night to the extended club-mix of *Is This The Way To Amarillo?*

Round 5 and Magic is pulling some neat tricks out of the bag. If this is FIGHT SKOOL then Magic was the head boy. He's got fast hands and the Rat is slowing. He keeps covering up and leaning back on the ropes. He's looking tired and Magic can sense it. He steps up a gear and every punch is connecting. It's getting noisy in there.

And that's another thing.

No one warns you about the noise that boxing makes. Magic was hitting the Rat with a lot of shots. Left hooks, straight rights, double jabs, combinations, they were all hitting home. When you hear that sickening smack of leather on skin you never forget it. It sounds like nothing else.

SMACK.

And then there's the grunts.

UHFF.

And the squeal and scratch of boxing boots on canvas. There's the trainer and the cut-man shouting from the corner:

MOVE.

STICK HIM.

CUT THE RING OFF.

WORK THE BODY.

The noise of it, the smell, the camera man mopping up the slop with a towel: you don't get that on Pay-Per-View. Boxing on telly is skimmed milk, all the cream has been taken out. When you watch boxing in your front room with a pizza and a can of Carlsberg, then you watch something else: a sport that's only loosely related to boxing, kind of its third cousin by marriage. Telly boxing is stardust and glitter. It's all silk robes and leopard skin shorts. It's showbiz. To experience the real thing you really have to be there at ringside. You have to hear the punches and smell the hurt. Just watching live boxing is a painful business.

Not that you have to tell the Rat. He'd had enough and didn't come out for the 7th. He showed a lot of heart but in the ring heart alone isn't enough, you have to use everything you've got and then find some more from somewhere. Boxing is all about self communication: your heart, mind and body have to work as one. Arms, legs, shoulders, fists, they all have to pull together, your feet have to talk to each other. The Rat was in trouble. His feet weren't on speaking terms.

One hour later and I'm on the train home listening to the mini tape recorder I took to the fight. I'm looking for atmosphere and all I'm getting is screams, shrieks and whoops. It sounds like a cross between a mass murder and Ancient Rome. One female voice kept coming through:

Finish it.

Kill him.

C'mon Magic rip his spine out.

I was getting funny looks from the other passengers so I clicked off the tape. I sat back and looked at my reflection in the window.

Rip his spine out?

Blimey.

Brown Envelopes

The little man in the black suit meant business. He had a thick Irish accent and used it to talk quickly and quietly.

Eh? I said.

He kept looking around, licking his lips and tapping his nose. He looked like one of those *suits-you-sir* tailors off The Fast Show. He put his hand in his pocket and pulled out a brown envelope.

Here, he said, this'll look after you, so it will.

I took it off him.

The little man looked at me. He held his hand out.

Just a drink for the head boy, he said.

For an envelope?

Ah now, just a drink.

Now here comes the bit I can't understand. For some reason I put a fiver in his hand. I don't know why. I knew what I was doing, I was wide awake and as sober as I get, but I couldn't stop myself. It was a reflex action, like my hand didn't belong to me. The little man started to shuffle away.

Be lucky, he said.

I looked down at the brown envelope in my hand. It was a normal ten-for-a-quid everyday envelope. No big deal. By the time I looked up again the little man in the black suit had disappeared.

The Crombie was making itself at home. It swanned around Pontefract Races like it owned the place. I gave it free rein, it knew what it was doing. It turned me into an old hand, a pro-punter. I went around saying things like *good fetlocks* and *damn fine filly*. I got so carried away I nearly shelled out for a black woollen trilby from the Soopahats stall. Other horsey types looked at me and nodded. I nodded back. We shared smiles like we were sharing secrets. I leaned over the paddock fence and tried to earwig on their conversations. It was easy talk, horsey words from horsey mouths. The sound of North Yorkshire. Cut them in half and you'd see Malton, Thirsk and Ripon running through them like names through a stick of rock. They knew their stuff though. No doubt about it. They talked about weights and form and favourites and furlongs. They knew the names of all the jockeys and probably had them over for tea and biscuits. They spoke to bookies on two hundred quid mobiles. They understood the laws of chance and knew the maths behind the starting prices. They knew how the ground was running and whether the horse would make the trip. They knew about this and that and they knew about the other. Me? I knew nothing. I was clueless.

Time to open the envelope.

I bought a warm can of Carling in the Riders Bar and found a seat in the corner. I looked around. I don't know why. It just felt right. I put the envelope on the table. It looked at me and dared me to open it. I opened it. Inside, handwritten on a scrap of paper, were the words:

3rd RACE. No. 3. 5th RACE. No. 11

I opened the Racing Post and gave the gee-gees the once over. I had a mouthful of lager and thought about the little man in the black suit. Be lucky, he'd said. *Be lucky*. That was it. Go with it. I polished off the Carling and left the bar. I'd found my horses now all I needed was a bookie.

Parts of Pontefract Racecourse could do with a touch of TLC, either that or a big vat of creosote. It came across as somewhere between an army barracks and a 1950s Butlins. I didn't know whether to stand-by-my-bed or say *Morning Campers*. I leaned against the chip-van and looked across to the M62 and the cooling towers beyond. The motorway was getting on with itself and the cooling towers were busy smudging the sky. They looked like a cloud factory. From where I stood the clouds looked like they were going down, back into the towers. That's a neat trick, like making the steam go back into the kettle. I clocked all the on-course bookies, all those skinny fingers making fat money. I remember my mate Amos telling me he knew this bookie called Jack Crap. I wanted to find him. I wanted to go up to him and say – *Hello, are you Crap?* But Jack was having the day off. He was probably quaffing champagne cocktails in York. A bookie once told me that nothing is impossible, only improbable. I asked him to tell me the next winner of the Grand National. He looked at me and sniffed.

Impossible, he said, and then he told me the rules:

1.   When the odds are bigger than 6/1 go each way.
2.   Never chase your money. When it's gone, it's gone. Although strictly speaking, it hasn't really *gone*. Not in a gone-and-disappeared-into-the-ether-and-never-coming-back sense of the word. That money still exists somewhere, just not in your somewhere.
3.   Always smile, especially when you're losing. It confuses the bookies.
4.   Don't bet.

The third horse in the third race was called Vicars Destiny. I didn't like the name. It didn't do anything for me. Besides anything to do with vicars is always bit suspect in my book but the envelope knows best. I found a bookie called Mr Bradford and put a twenty on it to win. It didn't.

Back to the bar.

The barman looked like he'd been put together out of leftover bits and pieces. His little girl's voice didn't match his big man's face and his long thin arms didn't go with his short fat fingers. As for his nose, that was on its own. It looked like someone had thrown it at his face and it had just stayed put. I asked him if he had any tips.

Don't touch the bitter, he said.

The man sitting at the end of the bar had wirewool hair and a thick black moustache that was somewhere between a Saddam Hussein and a Groucho Marx. He had three full pints in front of him and a lot more inside him. His shirt was unbuttoned and so was his face. He threw me a wink in slow-mo. I threw one back.

Yesh, he slurred to no one, I'm fifty today.

His mate came over and slapped him on the back.

Never mind Alan, he said, think positive.

Thing poshitif?

Yeah, his mate said, I mean at least now you're too old to die young.

Alan stared at his beer.

Silly bashtard, he said.

I learnt to count watching the racing. I'd sit there on the psychedelic 60s carpet in our front room and count the jockeys who fell off. There was no CBeebies in those days. That's why I'm rubbish at maths, to me numbers equal pain. To this day, whenever I count up to ten, I get images of little blokes in silk shirts wincing about with broken collarbones and bruised ribs.

Race five was the *4.10 Wakefield Unison Quality Services For Quality People Handicap (Class C).* Horse number 11 was Double Vodka. Sounded good, like a winner. Double Vodka was in form and had won its last two races at Doncaster and Ripon. I went to give Mr Bradford some more money.

The horses set off and people started shouting. They shouted at the horses, they shouted at the jockeys, and they shouted at each other. When the riders turned into the home straight things got really loud. The bloke behind me sounded like he was going to bust. He must have put his house on it.

Come on will yer, give it some bloody leather.

Bring it home lad.

Let it go, for God's sake, let it go. Please.

Double Vodka didn't need God's help. It romped home at 4/1. I was quids in. The envelope was working.

Mr Bradford's fingers were used to money and he counted out my winnings without looking. Bookies' money is always grubby but it still felt good. When I went back into the Riders Bar there was only one drink I could buy.

Double Vodka, I said to the man with the thrown-on nose, and have one yerself.

Cheers, he said in his little girl's voice.

There was a lot of money being blown in the bar. Fivers, tenners, twenties and fifties, straight from the bookies pockets, were flying all over the place. What chance have you got? If the bookies don't get you, then the breweries will. I took the Crombie off and looked around. In one corner of the bar, scribbling into a notebook, was a little man in a black suit. I did a bit of a comedy double-take but it was him alright.

The Envelope Man.

I picked the Crombie up and made my way across to his table. By the time I got there he'd vanished. *Again.* How does he do that? He should be on the telly. Ah well. I raised my glass and toasted his empty chair.

Be lucky, I said to it, be lucky.

Pocket Size

When Hilda met The Queen

Two old dears are having a chinwag outside the Sit-a-While greasy spoon on the corner of Broad Lane in Huddersfield. Both are talking at the same time. One of them is the bargain basement version of Queen Victoria: black hat, black scarf, black everything. The other is the spit of Hilda Baker. Lots of tutting, shaking of heads and sighing is going on. Queen Vic is sucking on a king-size like it's her last request and Hilda can't move for Morrison's carrier bags crammed full of bent tins and 2-for-1 offers. The sky is a holiday brochure blue. Even though it's a warm dry day, both are wearing thick winter coats. As I pass I hear this conversation.

Anyway pet, I best be going. He'll only start off if I don't get back.

Oh I know, OK then, I'll see you later.

Right y'are, sweetheart.

Hey.

What?

Mind that dog shit love.

Old people. They're not what they used to be.

Eating Rick Stein

Let's get the Yorkshire pudding out of the way.

For a start it belongs to us, it's got Yorkshire in its name. When it comes to telling you where it's from the Yorkshire pudding isn't backward at coming forward. Oh no. The Yorkshire pudding makes an ordinary dinner extraordinary. If you have one for a starter you feel different. Suddenly you're eating a three course meal. Suddenly you're posh.

The Yorkshire pudding can do impressions. It's a culinary chameleon. It can be a starter, a main course or a pudding. Everyone has their own way of eating one, their own style.

Dad sprinkled sugar on his, four or five spoonfuls, no wonder his teeth fell out. Nanan had currants in hers, like a spotted dick, and I had it with gravy on. I liked the crunchy burnt black bits on the rim and the way you could make a gravy puddle on the soggy stuff in the middle. You could pour some gravy on the outside, all the way round the Yorkshire pudding, and make a moat. That was the way to eat one. That way the Yorkshire pudding became a castle on your plate.

Mum knew all about the magic of flour, eggs and milk. She knew about batter, about sifting and beating. Mum knew about getting the oven piping hot and about eating the Yorkshires as soon as they came out, before they went limp and tragic. Mum never used to say the pudding bit. She'd say – *Do you want a Yorkshire for dinner?* We knew what she meant. I'd always say yes.

How many?

I'd think about it for a bit, feel my belly, see if it felt empty.

Two Yorkshires please, I'd say.

I was chuffed I had a Mum who was good at making Yorkshires, a Mum who knew the secrets. I always got two, even if my belly didn't feel empty. I always found room. Yorkshire is the biggest county in England, you had to have a big belly to fit two in.

Dad's told me, loads of times, about the greasy spoons he used to eat in when he was on the road. He just reels them off. There was the Shepherd's Rest in Ripponden. That was a good one. It was run by a bloke called Cyril who did a good pie and gravy. There was Greasy Joe's in Sheffield, the Redhouse in Doncaster, the Flying Sausage and the Boot and Shoe in Leeds. Dad was a professional eater. His favourite transport café was a place called the Tomato Dip on the old road into Skipton. That was the place. Whenever he was passing he'd nip in for a dripping tea-cake. It'd come still warm, he told me, when yer bit into it the fat dripped down yer chin.

Mmmmmmm.

Dad had this big chipped pint pot. He held it like a trophy and drank his tea out of it. Sometimes he slurped really loudly, and we'd all laugh but Mum didn't. He'd stop doing it then. When his pot was full you'd see the tea leaves floating about on the top. They looked like bits of wood or dead midgies. Dad sometimes gave me a drink out of it. The tea tasted sweet and warm and was always nicer than mine. There was a picture of a ship on the front of the pot. It was an old tall ship, like the Cutty Sark or something. The sea was a bit choppy and the ship was having a hard time. There were some sailors shouting at each other. They didn't look happy. I think they were swearing. On the back of Dad's pint pot was a poem:

Sweet oh sweet is that sensation
When two hearts in union meet
But the pain of separation
Mingles bitter with the sweet.

The pint pot was there at every dinner and every tea. I got to know the ship, the sailors and the poem on the back off by heart. I never knew what the sailors had to do with the poem. I couldn't work that one out. Imagine being on a ship in a stormy sea, the waves are getting bigger and bigger and suddenly you start swanning about going *Sweet oh sweet is that sensation.* Yeah, that's just what you need. You'd get your head kicked in. Once in school Ms Cowersley asked if we knew any poems. I took a breath and said the pint pot one aloud. It took bottle but I got through it. Ms Cowersley smiled and asked me where I'd read it.

In a book Miss.

It's beautiful Craig, Ms Cowersley said, what's it called?

I shrugged. On the outside I was trying to be all cool and unbothered but on the inside my head was going doolally.

Thinkthinkthinkthink.

I had a brainwave.

It's called *The Sailor's Farewell* Miss.

I got a gold star.

I was in love with Ms Cowersly, lying to her was the least I could do.

At school though, dinners were different things. There were queues and dining halls, rules and regulations. There were 1st and 2nd sittings and dinner ladies. One of the dinner ladies looked like the Wicked Witch of the West: hook-nose, long hair, crooked fingers. I gave her a wide berth. Worst of all was the teacher on dining room duty. Mrs Brooksby had hair like Marge Simpson and never missed a trick. If she saw you mashing your roast spuds into the gravy you'd be in for it. She'd snatch the fork out of your hand and tell you, in a really loud Teacher-Telling-Off voice, that mashing wasn't allowed - *Not in this school, laddie.* Neither was mixing the dollop of jam you got with the rice pudding. Strawberry was the best. You'd stir it all up and get a bowl of shocking pink goo. It looked good, like space food for aliens, but if Mrs Brooksby saw it you got the old Teacher-Telling-Off routine again.

Not in this school, laddie.

Debbie had black shiny hair and white shiny teeth and looked like Betty Rubble.

I fell for her bigtime.

She was my first proper girlfriend. By girlfriend I mean woman, by woman I mean she didn't have a paper-round. She laughed at all my crap jokes and made me feel like Groucho Marx, Oliver Hardy and Eric Morecambe all rolled into one. Mr Funnyman. We'd do that young lovers thing and stare at each other for ages without speaking. We did it on buses, in pubs, anywhere. We'd try to see into each other's souls. I didn't know what a soul looked like but I did it anyway. I did it because Debbie wanted me to. I'd watch Eastenders because Debbie wanted me to. I'd go shopping on Saturday afternoons because Debbie wanted me to. When she wanted me to take her out to a posh restaurant, all she had to do was click her fingers and that was it, I'd do it.

And I did it.

Gianni's was on Bingley Road in Shipley. Everything about it was soft: the lights, the music, the chairs. I think the place was made out of cushions. It had candles on the tables, red roses in fancy vases and a wine list. There was a blackboard on the wall telling you all about Today's Specials and something called Soup of the Day. It all seemed a bit vague. Why not just say tomato soup and leave it at that? Gianni's was a mysterious world, out to trick me at every turn. I had to be on my guard. It all went downhill when I saw the menu. It was full of words I'd never seen before. They were all in French or Italian. You had to be some kind of bilingual Columbo to figure it out. What the hell was Steak au Poivre? I worked the steak bit out but what's au Poivre when it's at home? What was Prosciutto and Mozzarella? They sounded like lovers from one of those operas they show on BBC2. As for Boeuf Bourguignon, well, that just reminded me of 1987.

Let me explain.

Back then I got the sack from a factory in Halifax that made fitted kitchen units. No violins thanks, I was happy about it. Over the moon in fact, eight hours a day on a glue-gun is enough for anybody. Anyway, the big boss man called me into his office and said that he was sacking me for insubordination.

I looked at him.

What? I said.

Insubordination, he said again.

That's not fair, I said, you can't sack me for something I can't spell.

It was the same with Boeuf Bourguignon. In fact it was worse. Never mind spelling it, I couldn't even say the word. Berf-ber-gin-yor. Barf-bog-gig-noy. Forget it. I was out of my depth, way out. I sounded like a cross between Inspector Clouseau and Jacques Chirac. I didn't know food could be so complicated.

I had to do something. Debbie was looking at me and I had to make a move. I ran my finger down the menu and took pot luck. I was pinning the tail on the donkey. I could have ordered anything: snails, oysters, bulls balls, you name it. I got lucky. I ended up with a plate full of Chicken Chasseur.

It was a first. I was eating food made with wine, with *vin*. I never got this at home. Apart from the Christmas pudding and the odd sherry trifle, Mum never put booze in the food we ate. I can't remember eating Yorkshire pudding lightly sautéed in a rich brandy sauce. And yet here I was, sitting in a plush restaurant full of soft lights and fat cushions, staring into my cartoon girlfriend's soul and stuffing my face with chicken in a red wine sauce with pan-fried shallots and button mushrooms. Every mouthful took me somewhere else, somewhere where the lights were softer and the cushions fatter. Softer, fatter, softer, fatter. It was like eating a dream - *Sweet oh sweet is that sensation.*

And I never wanted to wake up.

Go to Neal Street in Bradford, follow your nose and you come to the Karachi Restaurant. Perhaps the word restaurant is stretching it a bit, *restaurant* makes you think of waiters in crispyclean white shirts and black dicky bows. It's not that kind of place. Let's just call it the Karachi and leave it at that. It was here in the early 80s that I had my first curry. It was a moment I haven't forgotten. Your first curry is a memory up there with your first pint, your first wage packet and your first kiss. It's a BIG first. If you think about it, tackling a mean looking chicken rogan josh for the first time is a bit like losing your virginity: you're nervous, you're unsure about what to do, you don't know where to start and you only hope that you finish the job without embarrassing yourself. The only difference I can see is that when you eat a curry you keep your pants on. Or at least I do, but maybe that's just me.

Eating my first curry was the end of something and the start of something else. For the first time in my life I was eating food that my Mum and Dad wouldn't touch with a bargepole. No liver and onions, no cold meat and chips on Mondays and definitely no Yorkshires. Nowadays my old man wolfs down his lamb bhunas like, well like a wolf, but back then it was something that he just didn't do. He didn't get the chance. Mum and Dad never went out for a meal. If they did it would be someone's wedding anniversary or birthday do. And then the food would be steak and chips if they were lucky or sausage rolls if they weren't. Going out for a curry with your mates was a real independent, man-about-town, grown-up thing to do. It was a step inside another world where everything was different: the food, the wallpaper, the smells, *especially* the smells. Even the words smelt good.

To order a meal in the Karachi wasn't just to order a meal, it was to speak another language. You had to get your tongue round words that it had never been round before, your mouth ended up feeling like it belonged to someone else. In the Karachi food was made with cardamom, cumin, cinnamon, garam masala, tumeric, coriander and saffron. What was going on here? These weren't things you made food with, not to me. These were the names of angels, pixies or witches' cats.

Come here Saffron my pretty, there's a good girl.

You got crisps as big as your plate called poppadoms and bread without butter called chapattis. This was living, just saying those words made me feel like the genie out of *Aladdin*. Poppadum, chapatti, poppadum, chapatti. I felt like I was granting someone three wishes.

Alakhazam!

Then came the curries themselves: rogan josh, jalfrezi, bhuna, dopiaza and vindaloo. Surely this is not food. You don't expect me to put something that sounds so not-from-round-here, so other-worldly in my mouth do you? Where I come from food is called fish and chips, cottage pie or Yorkshire pudding. Rogan josh and vindaloo are names for explorers or mountaineers. Those brave sailors on Dad's pint pot probably had names like that. We're talking about real men here. Men who look like Brian Blessed and fight lions before breakfast, men who wrestle bears for the hell of it and win. Men who go all the way to the North Pole and back wearing just one jumper. *Just one.* Captain Rogan Josh and Admiral Vindaloo: big men, big beards, big lives.

Rick Stein, from the BBC programme *Food Heroes,* came up to Bradford to do a feature on the Karachi. Rick, who looks like everybody's favourite uncle, was well pleased and wandered around looking like the cat that nicked the cream. To mark his visit there is now a dish called the Rick Stein. It's really a lamb and spinach balti in disguise. The last time I was there I ordered it. I had to. It's not everyday you get to eat a TV chef.

And very nice he was too.

Drinking Sam Webster

It's October 1974 and Ali is fighting big George in the Jungle. The Greatest is leaning back on the ropes and George is letting him have it.

Big left.

Big right.

Big left again.

The bombs just keep on coming.

Dad keeps throwing quick, snatchy left jabs at the telly and shouting a lot. He's doing that grunting thing that boxers do.

Uhff

Uhff.

Uhff.

He looks pretty sharp. Dad's drinking Webster's Green Label and enjoying it, really enjoying it. He's making those big wet look-at-me-I'm-really-enjoying-it noises. I'm drinking the stuff and I'm not enjoying it. I'm trying to but I can't. Not a bit. It smells funny and tastes like it's gone off. I'd rather have a glass of milk or some dandelion and burdock, even some American cream soda would be better. But I stick with it. It's worth it. It's past midnight, I've got a ringside seat and I'm drinking beer with Dad.

I'm ten years old.

The drinks cabinet in our house was in the bottom cupboard of the Welsh dresser. The Welsh dresser was Mum's pride and joy. It was big and chunky and took up half the dining room. To me the Welsh dresser wasn't a big deal, it was just a suped-up sideboard with shelves. But Mum liked it and that was that. When it first came we all got a lecture about being careful, I mean *really* careful. This is not a table, Mum said, do not put hot cups of tea on it. Somebody wasn't careful enough because a week later the dresser had a big, horrible, guilty looking, tea-cup-sized stain on it. We got another lecture but nobody owned up. Mum and Dad went around with I'm-not-impressed faces. They tutted and sighed and said things like – *You've let me down the lot of you* – and - *You can't have owt nice in this bloody house.* It all got a bit cloak and dagger. People looked at each other but said nothing. It was like living in an episode of *Miss Marple*. To this day I don't know who did it. In the end Mum had enough and hid the stain with a vase. Case closed. The culprit remains at large.

When she wasn't investigating domestic mysteries, Mum used to fill the dresser's shelves with plates, the posh ones that you never ate your dinner off, not even at Christmas. These were never proper plates to me, just ornaments doing a spot of moonlighting. Mum had loads: big plates, small plates, round plates, square plates, cups and saucers. There were some blue Japanese willow pattern ones that told a story, something about a boy and a girl, a bridge and a bird. I don't know how it went. Maybe that's why you didn't use these plates at dinner-time. You'd be so busy trying to suss out what the boy and girl were up to, that you'd forget all about your fish fingers. I don't know.

In the booze cupboard – drinks cabinet was always pushing it a bit - all the classics were there. There was some rum and brandy that belonged to Dad, some sherry and whisky that belonged to Mum and some banana liqueur stuff that belonged to anybody who wanted to risk it. Nobody did. It smelt like monkey sick. Dad's Green Label though, didn't live in the dresser cupboard. It preferred its own company and had its own little spot in the kitchen at the side of the fridge. It stood there next to sacks of spuds and cabbages and pop bottles. The Green Label seemed happy enough. It never complained. I don't really know why the Green Label never made it into the booze cupboard but I have a theory.

And here it is.

To open the booze cupboard you had to have a reason: Christmas, New Year's Eve, England winning something, that type of thing. But Dad could walk into the kitchen willy-nilly, whenever he wanted, I mean it was only a kitchen. People didn't have to be holding hands at midnight and singing *Auld Lang Syne* for him to crack open a cheery bottle or two. Green Label had no airs and graces - what you saw is what you got. It was working beer.

The bottles Green Label came in were small, stubby and looked to me like those in the song *Ten Green Bottles.* You know the one:

> *Ten green bottles, hanging on the wall*
> *Ten green bottles, hanging on the wall*
> *and if one green bottle should accidentally fall*

Webster's Green Label was the first beer I ever saw and the first I ever tasted. It was made just down the road from us at Ovenden Wood, a couple of miles out of Halifax. The brewery's still there, half Disney castle, half Colditz, but they don't make the beer there anymore. John Smith's in Tadcaster does the honours these days. Like I say, I wasn't really a fan but Green Label must have been doing something right if it makes me start singing just by thinking about it.

I'm on the road to Booze. No really I am. I'm not going to get all News of the Worldy on you here and bang on about my battle with the bottle – *Yorkshireman In Alco Hell* – I'm just telling you what I'm doing, and what I'm doing is driving to Booze.

I turn off the A1, always a good idea, and pass through Aiskew, Bedale, Patrick Brompton, Constable Burton and Leyburn. It's like flicking through a coffee table book called *The Hidden Villages of Yorkshire.* Around Bellerby I pass the military shooting ranges and the – Caution! Tank Drivers Under Instruction - signs. I keep going, moving targets are harder to hit, and drive through Fremington where old ladies sit with Labradors in cars waiting for the rain to stop.

It doesn't.

Booze is just above Langthwaite, north of Reeth. It would be. Places like Booze are always north of somewhere.

I pull up in Langthwaite outside the Red Lion. The Red Lion is what the tourist brochure people like to call sleepy looking, either that or it's slipped into a coma. Booze is up a steep tractor track-cum-road-cum-mudslide called Scotty Hill. This is it. This is what I've come for. I put the Crombie on, take a deep breath and strike out.

As far as I could make out Booze is a couple of farms carved into the hillside, a fistful of pheasants and not a lot else. It has big views of Great Pinseat, Calver Hill and St Mary's Church but that's about it. I wasn't disappointed, not at all. I could smell coal-fires and see forever. I leant against a lime scarred dry stone wall and started thinking.

I was thinking about the little varnished wooden plaque that we had on the wall at home. We got it from a seafront shop in Scarborough or somewhere. It had *Work is the Curse of the Drinking Classes* written on it and a picture of a red-nosed bloke wearing a flat cap. Above him was a speech bubble with the word *HIC!*

I was thinking about how Mum used to say druffen instead of drunk. She'd say – *Did you come home druffen last night?* - and – *Look at that druffen bugger.* I never got that. But then again Mum used to say waggin instead of wagon and I never got that either.

And I was thinking about the first time I got *druffen* on my mate Sucker's homebrew. Sucker's mum and dad ran the Bradshaw Tavern in Halifax so he reckoned he was bit handy on the beer-making front. He wasn't.

His beer looked like pond water and had stuff floating in it, but it did the job. Too right it did. The next morning I was a bonafide, newly signed-in, fully-paid up member of the Hangover Club.

HIC!

I'm in the grounds of Christ Church in Mount Pellon, Halifax. In front of me is the biggest grave in the graveyard. It has prime position and is slap-bang in front of the Church's stained-glass window. Whoever it belongs to did the right things and knew the right people. The gravestone is an impressive looking affair with pillars, roses and angels and looks like a scaled down version of the Scott Memorial on Princes Street in Edinburgh. The grave itself might show off a bit but the words on the headstone tell it like is:

In memory of Samuel Webster
Born Sep 3 1813
Died May 5 1872

There he is. The man who made the beer that made Dad smack his lips, the man whose beer brought me here. Samuel Webster: the man himself.

Sam's grave has been left alone too long and is losing the battle against brambles, nettles and dock leaves. I was just about to roll up my sleeves and have a go at it when some well turned out, shiny people started arriving for a wedding. I knew it was a wedding because they all had that let's-get-this-over-with-and-get-to-the-boozer expression that wedding guests tend to go in for. I got a few who-the-hell's-that-bloke kind of looks and thought I'd best be on my way. As *Here Comes The Bride* piped up I cleared away some weeds and a couple of old crisp packets. After all this *was* Samuel Webster, the man whose Green Label makes me sing when I think about it.

Pocket Size

The Ursa Major Man

I'm sitting on a bench opposite Debenhams in Kirkgate, Leeds. I'm eating a packet of Walker's Cheese and Onion and I'm listening to a busker. He's good. He sounds like Sting. He's got an amp on a handcart that's hooked up to a car battery and he's singing a song called *Clearing Out The Cobwebs*. When I dropped a handful of pocket shrapnel into his guitar case, he gave me a weird kind of half-smile. I don't know if it meant Thank You or Tight Bastard. Either way he was worth it. *Clearing Out The Cobwebs* was catchy, very catchy. I was humming it all day.

Next to me is an old bloke leaning on his walking stick watching some skateboarders. One of the skateboarders, a teenager who was all arms and legs and nothing in-between, lost control on a tricky 360 and sent his skateboard bolting towards the old man. It startled him, knocking the stick out of his hand. He kicked the skateboard back and looked at me.

Ursa Major, he said.

I offer him a crisp but he wasn't interested.

Ursa Major, he said again.

Later on, I'm sitting on the back steps at home. I'm thinking about the stars. I look up and see Orion winking at me. He's looking sharp tonight. Big shoulders, glam rock belt, bow and arrow. He should be a dab-hand with the old quiver sticks by now, he's been practising for donkey's. From here it looks like he's using the chippy on Broad Lane as a bullseye. Cassiopeia is nailed to the sky directly above the ridge tiles I re-pointed last summer. Some nights the moon looks like it's been cannon-balled straight out of the chimney.

The front steps tell a different story. A tin rattles out a mini timpani down the street while a cat pulls yoga stretches on a wheelie bin lid. The Great Bear drags the Plough over Ravensknowle Park and Tolson Museum, where he stamps his big question mark in the sky. I just want to know what he's asking.

Lions and Rabbits

The sky rang a bell. I'd seen that colour before somewhere. It was blueygreen and looked warm. I wanted to touch it. It was seaweed and heather, it was yesterday's teabags and dog blankets, it was slate and old people's carpets, it was something else but I couldn't place it. Not to worry, it'll come.

For years I thought Leeds didn't exist. To me it was just another name for a football team. And not a great name either. It sounds too much like tweeds, swedes and weeds. Let's face it, it's not a name that's going to put the wind up the other team. But there it was alongside teams with proper names like Rovers and Rangers, Hotspur and Albion, Wolves and Wanderers, City and Town.

Leeds. Leeds. Leeds.

I'd hear the football results on Saturday tea-time.

Leeds United 2, Somebody Else 0.

Somebody Else 0, Leeds United 2.

And that was that, football stuff. It's not that we were anti-Leeds in our house it's just that we never went. We didn't need to. If Mum wanted to head for the bright lights of the big city then I'd be told to wash my neck, put on my best flowery shirt and get dragged around Bradford. That was the place, the Big B, the first city I ever saw. Bradford had a Cathedral, a university and proper shops like BHS, C&A and Littlewoods. Going to Bradford was a big deal. It had multi-storey car parks and different coloured buses. It had something called a precinct and shops with lifts called department stores. Some were so big they had their own cafes. Some of them even had magic, automatic doors, straight out of *Tomorrow's World,* that whooshed open without being touched.

WHOOSH.

The sound of the future. Bradford was an adventure, a wonderland, a taste of what was to come.

And then there was Leeds.

The Dark Arches, down on Granary Wharf, is a good place to start. The Arches is an echoey underworld full of art galleries and noodle bars, craftshops and designer boutiques. Trains rumble above and the Aire blunders below. It's a half-way place alive with shadows and secrets and comes across as somewhere between a funfair ride and the Batcave. Tannoys were playing a piece of public artwork called *Soundlines* by Bill Montana. Mr Montana mixed live sounds from the river and the train station to create his cutting edge masterpiece. Now don't get me wrong, I'm all for people doing wacky things and being a bit arty. I know what *Soundlines* was trying to do. It was out to create a mood, a tone and to give the Dark Arches a voice. Fair enough, good luck to it. I'm afraid it didn't do it for me. *Soundlines* was just too full of groans, grunts and gurgles to be believable. It sounded like the Devil brushing his teeth.

I left Satan to his oral hygiene and blinked my way back into the sun. Down on the canal basin narrow-boats called *Hanley's Pride, Cambrian* and *Camelot II* were moored up taking a breather. People sat on the grass reading *The Sun* and drinking Orangina. There was a German Shepherd licking himself the way dogs do and everyone pretended not to be watching him. I stood on a little stone bridge and looked at the red brick buildings. They all looked the same. They're faceless and don't even have proper names. They're called things like BMB, UKI, KPMG and BT. All these letters started to swirl about and gave me a headache. It was time to take five, step back and head for the river.

Mark, my brother, has talent, real talent. I'm not talking about playing the violin or being a bit of a dinkywiz on the football pitch. I'm talking about the kind of talent that comes from a different place, from deep inside somewhere. For a start he can whistle with any combination of fingers. Index finger and ring finger? No problem. Little pinky and thumb? Piece of cake. He can blow these loud, long, piercing whistles that spook dogs and sound like a car alarm going off inside your head. He can also burp on cue. Mum was never too impressed with that one but I was. Mark did the big brother bit. He sat me down and gave me lessons on the noble art of belching. He told me it's something to do with swallowing air and lodging it in that hollow bit behind your Adam's apple.

Don't let it touch your lungs, he'd say.

I tried, failed and tried again. It's no use. I don't understand how my throat works.

Mark has another neat party trick.

SwaleUreNiddWharfeAireCalderDerwentDon.

He just came out with it one day. I thought he was having some kind of thrombo. I asked him what it all meant.

Yorkshire rivers, he said.

Then he was off again.

SwaleUreNiddWharfeAireCalderDerwentDon.

Then, just because he can, he did it all backwards.

DonDerwentCalderAireWharfeNiddUreSwale.

Backwards and forwards. Forwards and backwards. How about that? My brother can make rivers go backwards. Now that is talent.

Rivers are complicated things. There are rivers and streams, becks and brooks, tributaries and creeks. There's something called a rivulet and something else called a runnel. Then, just to fuzzle things up a bit further, the river Humber, where most of the Yorkshire rivers end up, isn't really a river at all. It's an estuary. It comes and goes with the tide. It only calls itself a river because it doesn't want to be left out. The Humber is a slippery customer. It's out to trick us and pull a fast one. It's making sure we're paying attention.

The Aire though, doesn't care what we think. It goes its own way and is a bit of a loner. Whilst the Swale pals up with the Ure, and the Nidd and Wharfe get friendly with the Ouse, the Aire flows all the way from Airehead in Malham to the sea without so much as a kind word or a glance over its shoulder. If the Wharfe and the Swale are excitable and bubbly, then the Aire is a moody, Billy-no-mates. It's that bloke nobody really knows who turns up at parties, hangs around in the kitchen all night and then disappears without saying thanks for the trifle.

Miserable bugger.

The Pagans believed that when the new gods came along, the old ones took the hint and went into the rivers. I sat on the embankment for a while and stared deep into the Aire. I was looking for gods. I didn't see any. I saw crisp packets, a newspaper and a polystyrene fast food thingy and that was it. The gods must have been having a day off.

I walked under the railway bridge, towards the Scarbrough Hotel, and made my way around the corner to City Square. This is the place where the Black Prince meets the Majestyk nightclub, where James Watt meets the Bondi Beach Bar and where Dr Hook – that's the Vicar of Leeds 1837-1859 and not the bloke with the eye-patch singing about *Sylvia's Mother* – meets William Hill. There are statues everywhere around here. There is one of Joseph Priestley who was Minister at Mill Hill Chapel across the road from 1767 to 1773. It was Joseph who discovered oxygen, which kind of makes you wonder what the people of Leeds did before he made his little breakthrough. Did they stagger round City Square, all blue-faced and gasping saying, *Hey Joe, hurry it up with the oxygen will yer, I can't get a breath here.*

There was a big sign on the Chapel wall saying SANCTUARY FOR ALL. I tried the door. It was locked, so much for sanctuary then. As I stood there a bloke with half a sandwich saw me making notes and came up to me.

Are you sketching? he said.

I wish I was, I said back.

He looked at my notes and sniffed.

Y'know this place, he said and nodded towards the Chapel.

Yeah, I said.

It's always on *Songs of Praise*, he said, every other Sunday it's on the telly it is. The other places don't get a look in.

He looked straight at me.

Pisses me right off, he said.

Then he sniffed again and disappeared.

And so did I.

The sky was starting to bug me. I still couldn't place it. Moss, spring cabbage, pulped plums, my old school football socks? Nearly but not nearly enough.

Opposite the Chapel is Number One City Square. It's a massive office block with a funky glass lift like the kind you see on American super-duper skyscrapers. I've walked past a million times and always fancied a ride. Well, it was time to stop fancying and start doing. I stood outside for a while watching people come and go. They all had that I'm-at-work look about them. I put my on own I'm-at-work-as-well face and went into the lobby. I got straight into the lift and pressed the 10th floor. The lift took off and the city sprawled below me. It was a real *Charlie and the Chocolate Factory* moment. I had three rides before a security guard started giving me funny looks. The glass lift at City Square is the best ride in town. Do it and Leeds belongs to you.

I walked up Park Row past the banks, the Slug and Lettuce, Johnson's the Dry Cleaners, Caffe Nero, The Firefly Bar and made my way across the Headrow. People were sat on the stone steps in front of the Art Gallery munching away on dinner time butties. I felt like I'd stumbled into some kind of Big Sandwich Rock Festival. Speaking of rocks, I stood on a stone flag that had the words YOU ARE A ROCK cut into it. Fair enough, I've been called worse. In front of the library a big bloke and a little bloke were playing a game of chess on a super-size chess board. Some medium-sized people stood around watching. The big bloke was winning hands down. He took the little bloke's knight and bishop without the little bloke noticing. It didn't seem fair somehow. Maybe chess should be more like boxing and have different weight categories? I think the big bloke should at least have had some kind of handicap, one arm tied behind his back maybe, or a blindfold or something. That would even things up.

I like it. I like it a lot.

I'm talking about the Town Hall. Leeds Town Hall is *the* Town Hall, the best one in the country. I mean it. It's big and daft, magnificent and silly, beautiful and brash. The next time you walk past it start singing. Go on. You know you want to. If you're really lucky the big four ton bell in the clock-tower might even join in. If people stare at you then sod them and sing louder. What do you care? When you talk about Leeds Town Hall you're not talking about a building, a thrown together collection of rooms with a roof stuck on top. In fact you're not even talking about a Town Hall. Calling Leeds Town Hall a Town Hall doesn't even come close. You're talking about a work of art, a song and dance, an overture, a poem. You're talking about a moment caught in time, a dream come true, a vision, a quality of light. What you've got there is a living, breathing, walking, talking celebration of stone.

Celebrate good times, come on.

I told you I liked it.

Green tea, thistles, the scum on mill ponds, the covers on Shackleton's high seat chairs?

There's Chuck Berry, Charles Bronson, Charlie Brown, Cuthbert Broderick and me. Having the same initials always made me think us lot shared something. We could nod and wink at each other and nobody else would know why. I could rock and roll with Chuck, get mean with Charles and get animated with Charlie. I like being a CB. I'm in good company.

I know what you're thinking.

What about Cuthbert Broderick and who the hell is he?

Cuthbert had dreams and his dreams were made of stone. He was the man who dreamt up and designed Leeds Town Hall. It was his baby. I don't know what Cuthbert was on at the time but whatever it was it worked. And it didn't stop there. As well as the Town Hall he also designed the old public baths and the Civic Theatre on Cookridge Street and the oval-shaped Corn Exchange down by the market. Cuthbert was on a roll.

In front of the Town Hall there are four stone lions that keep watch over Victoria Square. They're as big as elephants and are starting to look their age. It suits them. Their crumbling faces make them look like something you'd find in an Egyptian museum. If you think about it that's what they are. All the great man-made structures in Yorkshire are the closest thing we've got to ancient monuments. The Corn and Wool Exchanges, the Castles and the Cathedrals, the Abbeys and Town Halls, those are our pyramids.

And just like the original pyramids they come with their own myths. I remember an old lady telling me about how the Town Hall lions come alive when there's a full moon. They get up, have a stretch and then roar at the stars. It's a good story and I wanted to find out more. There was a newspaper seller on the corner. I knew he was a newspaper seller because he was doing that shouting thing.

Yorker Po, Ger yer Yorker Po, Yorker Po.

He had an inky face and looked like he'd been selling papers all his life. I reckoned if anyone could tell me about the lions this was the man.

Scuse me, I said.

Yorker Po, he said back.

Do you know those lions on the Town Hall steps?

Yorker Po, he said again.

I pressed on.

Have you heard the story where they come alive when there's a full moon? I said.

Yorker Po, he said again.

I'll buy a paper thanks, I said.

That shut him up.

Lions coming alive, he said, pocketing my change, are you on summat? I think someone's been pulling your plonker mate.

Ah well. It's still a good story. I took my copy of the Yorker Po and said goodbye to the lions.

I'm in Ann Summers, up by the City Varieties on Land's Lane. I don't know why I'm in Ann Summers but I am. Let's just say I stumbled in and leave it at that. I'm speaking to Daniel.

So what's your biggest seller then?

The Rampant Rabbit, he said.

Eh?

Suddenly I felt like my Granddad.

Come here, he said.

Daniel took me over to the sex toys section of the shop. This is the place where you find things called Cock Rings, Lusty Lickers, Dirty Dolphins, Pocket Pleasers and little willy-shaped biscuits called Hob Knobs. Daniel got a Rampant Rabbit out of a box and stuck it in my hand.

It was a serious piece of kit. It was made from see-through heavy duty latex-type stuff and came with revolving head, little rubber rabbit ears and ball bearings. It looked like something a plumber might use to unblock your drains.

That's the Platinum model, he said. It's forty pounds and we sell loads. I've just sold two this morning.

I think Daniel was trying to sell one to me.

It comes with free lubricant and has seven functions, he said.

Seven? I said.

It was Granddad speaking again.

Daniel nodded.

Blimey, I said, can you brush your teeth with it?

I always make crap jokes when I'm standing in a public place holding a large vibrating sex toy.

Daniel ignored me.

The ladies know what they want, he said. Daniel didn't wink but he should have done.

He turned the Rabbit on for me.

That's the gentle vibration, he said, like a warm up.

Then he flicked another switch and things moved up a gear.

That's on pleasure mode now.

My hand was shaking and starting to go numb. I could feel pins and needles setting in. Other people in the shop started to look over and smirk. I looked back and tried to act like this was something I did everyday. Daniel turned the Rabbit off.

What do you think? he said.

Not for me, thanks, I said.

I was on my way out of the shop when Daniel shouted over to me.

We're doing a good deal on Edible Thongs today, any flavour you like. The Strawberry Shockers are flying out.

I took a rain-check on the offer but Daniel had planted a seed. Maybe I could do another book called Yorkshire in an Edible Thong. Now there's an idea.

I was standing at the bar in the White Rose pub in the train station mulling over a pint of Tetley's when it came to me. It was the coat, I thought, the bloody coat. That's where I'd seen it before. The sky was the colour of the Crombie.

Great Train Journeys

One

13:27 Huddersfield to Barnsley

The weather was showing off. First it was sunny, then it wasn't. Then it was windy, then it wasn't. Then it was sunny again. Hat off, hat on, hat off again. It was like the weather was auditioning for a part in the West End. It was running through a routine and trying too hard. Then, for the big finish, it started raining. I looked up. The clouds were the colour of bad teeth and the sky had Yorkshire written all over it. Hat on again.

I'm on a train. I'm all alone. I've seen the driver, the conductor and that's it. That's fine, I'm happy with me but here's the thing: if I'm all on my tod, then how come every time we stop somebody else gets off? How does that one work? Maybe we've entered the fourth dimension and interrupted the space-time continuum? Maybe the people getting off the train today are due to get off tomorrow and we've caught them up? Maybe I'm just sharing the train with a load of yesterday's shadows? Or maybe it's something to do with the weather? Yeah, that'll be it.

All the windows are steamed up. I didn't know I breathed so much. I have to keep wiping a peephole in mine. All I see are empty stations and cheesed off trees. I pick up the free paper, the *Metro* and flick through. I see the headline - *The Man Who Grew A New Jaw On His Back*. I'm full of admiration for the miracles of modern medicine but at the same time I'm thinking it must be hard work cleaning his teeth. He must have a toothbrush with a two-foot handle.

Finally, at Honley some real live 3D people got on. A family of three sat down and started reading magazines. They obviously had nothing to say to each other. Mum had *Hello,* the teenage son had *FHM* and the little girl had *The Simpsons.* Personally I'd go for Homer. Every time.

An old bloke sat down and started to eat a sandwich. It must have been a good one, he was chewing it all the way to Barnsley.

All the stations were starting to look the same: wrought iron benches, lattice fences and *MetroTrain* timetables. Only Brockholes stood out with its 1940s shop signs for Brook Bond Tea and Colman's Mustard. It looked like a bad sitcom. I could hear the canned laughter as we pulled into Stocksmoor.

A teenage girl with a *Barbie Is A Slut* T-shirt got on. On her arm was a tattoo that said RUDEGIRLS AREN'T EASY. Fair enough. I never said they were. When she saw me staring she looked at me like I owed her money. Why have a tattoo if you don't want anybody to look at it? Tattoos can be interesting things. They say a lot about a person. I used to work with this bloke called Frank who had Jimi Hendrix's autograph tattooed across his back. Nothing wrong with that except when you got up close, it looked like it said Tim Henman. Frank blamed Jimi for having sloppy handwriting. I'm the same. My signature looks like it says Greg Smelly. I'm OK with it but I get funny looks in banks.

If I got a tattoo I wouldn't mess about. No half measures for me. If I was a Rudegirl, I'd shave my hair off and get the world tattooed on my head. I'd be a walking globe and get a job in a circus. My nose would be where Ghana is, tucked away on the west coast of Africa. I'd have one eye in Iraq, the other in Bermuda and I'd smile all the way from Rio de Janero to Madagascar. I'd have one ear in the middle of the North Pacific and the other in Hong Kong. As for Halifax, Huddersfield, Leeds and all the rest, they'd be on that sacred spot, right in the middle of my forehead. That's the place, my own little Yorkshire bhindi.

I looked through my peephole and saw the Emley Moor mast sticking up like a big exclamation mark. The top of it was lost in the clouds as if the sky was trying to rub it out.

People on the west coast of Ireland used to call themselves the real Irish. They lived in bogs, had turf fires and used the old words. When they opened their mouths to speak, this warm, sugary music came out. Listening to them was like sitting in a big bathful of treacle. These people weren't playing at being Irish like the West Britons who swanned around talking English in Dublin. These were the real thing, the genuine article, the proper Irish.

It was the same with Barnsley. I used to feel that if you came from Barnsley then you were a proper Yorkshire person, that you were somehow more Yorkshire than I was. They had the pits, the strikes and King Arthur. The first time I heard someone from Barnsley talk I thought they were taking the mick out of me. They were doing what I did but more of it. It sounded like a stage version of Yorkshire, a put on. I couldn't believe they came from the same county as me. They could have come from Nottingham or Derby or Outer Mongolia. They might have been the same breed but they were definitely from a different tribe. I remember looking at a map and finding out that Yorkshire is the largest county in England. Easy. I wanted to jump up and down and shout my head off. I felt like I'd won something. I realised then that the county I was born in is a big old place and everyone in it is just as Yorkshire as everyone else.

Just saying Barnsley makes you sound like you were born there. Make that long lazy *AR,* hold it just behind the tongue and you'll be rhyming night with neet and light with leet before you know it. There's no doubt about it, if coal could speak it would have a Barnsley accent. Bloody reet it would.

And that's part of the problem. Barnsley is a single mum with three kids, it has baggage. It's where the myths started. The Yorkshire of clogs and flatcaps, of ferrets and whippets was born there. The *Trouble at t'mills* and the *Ee by gums* all writhed and slithered and crawled their way out of the slagheaps. They're still crawling today.

I know some people who think that Barnsley IS Yorkshire. They really do. They've seen the *Monty Python* Four Yorkshire Men sketch and suddenly they're experts – *well you were lucky* - they've sat through *Kes* and think everyone walks about talking like Mr Sugden, or Brian

Glover to you and me. In South Yorkshire I suppose that's exactly what they do. In the west we sound like Brian Glover on the phone to his bank manager. As for the north, well, they just sound like his bank manager.

Opposite Dodworth station is an industrial estate. There was a container with the word HOPE spraypainted down its side. And it was padlocked. *Padlocked.* HOPE is going nowhere.

We left HOPE behind when we crossed the M1 and pulled into Barnsley station. Two young lovers were hugging each other. It was still pouring down but they didn't care. They only had eyes for each other and looked like an Athena poster. The bloke's mobile rang.

Shit, he said, it's doin me friggin 'ead in this.

I don't remember that bit in *Brief Encounter.*

Two

10:39 Huddersfield to Halifax

In front of Huddersfield train station is a statue of Harold Wilson. Harry's not hanging about, look how he's standing. It's not a stance that says Look-At-Me-I'm-Important but one that says Look-At-Me-I'm-Going-to-the-George-Hotel-For-A-Quick-Pint. He's even got his hand in his pocket fishing for beer money. Bottom's up Harry, here's to you.

The little woman in the station shop looked me up and down.

Are you the fugitive? she said.

The what?

The fugitive, y'know, from the competition on *Real Radio?*

No.

Are you sure?

Fraid so.

Oh.

I was sorry to let her down but I was glad she asked - the fugitive - I felt like Harrison Ford.

The old lady was sat on a bench waiting for a train. She was wearing a pink flowery hat and giving a master class in smoking. Her fingers, her lips and her cigarette seemed to come together without moving. The cigarette knew where it was going, it was made for her mouth and became part of her. Watching her was like watching some kind of hypnotic mini ballet. Smoking might be bad for you but she was good at it. I don't know where she bought the pink flowery hat but she had grace, real grace, and you can't buy that.

Somebody had left a copy of yesterday's *Halifax Evening Courier* on a platform seat. The headline caught my eye - *BUS DRIVER KNOCKED OUT BY CONKER*. I was just glad to be on the train.

I moved from Halifax to Huddersfield years ago and going back is weird. Not weird in big *X Files* way, in fact, on the weird scale from 1 to 10 it's only about a 3. It's a casual, comfy kind of weirdness. Every street, every pub and shop has a ghost. Mum used to work on the market, in Watson's the Confectioners. She'd bring a bagful of all the things that they couldn't sell home with her. I walk past the market now and I think of broken buns and squashed apple pies. There's a record shop called Bradley's Records on Market Street. I used to impress my mates and tell them that the shop belonged to my Uncle Frank. It worked.

Really? they said.

Oh yeah, I said, smugging it up, he's got another shop in Bradford and one in Leeds. I can get any record I want.

I clicked my fingers.

Just like that, I said.

Brillo.

Yeah, brillo.

I don't have an Uncle Frank, I never did. But every time I walk past Bradley's Records I think of him. Good old Frank. I wonder what he's doing with himself these days.

Then, when I'd had enough of lying to my mates, I started going into pubs: the Union Cross, the Sportsman, the Pot O'Four and the Vaults. There are about 60,000 pubs in Britain and it seemed that half of them were in Halifax. The best one though was the Upper George.

The George was a dark, dingy, smelly hole full of bikers and hippies trying their best to cling onto the 70s. They'd all stand in the corners smoking spliffs and grooving to *The Dark Side of the Moon* and *Stairway to Heaven*. The bitter in the George tasted like something you'd clean your floor with, your shoes stuck to the carpet and the toilet was straight out of *Trainspotting*. I didn't care. The George was the place to be.

Now and again though, we'd try the other pubs in town. I met my now ex-wife in the White Horse, had the wedding knees-up in Maggie McFly's and the divorce do in the Plummet Line. Not on the same day you understand. I walk through Halifax now and I walk through my own history, the good and the bad. Every street has a story, every pub a tale. It's all there mapped out before me.

When I left Halifax for Huddersfield some of my mates took it personally. I was letting them down. I was quitting and walking away. I don't know what I was quitting or walking away from, but that's how they made me feel. The fact I was only moving over the hill didn't matter, not in the slightest. I might as well have shaved my head, given everything to Oxfam and gone to live in Tibet. It was the fact I was leaving my home town that got to them, leaving the place where I'd lived for 30 years. The place where I was born, grew up, went to school, got a job and learned to drink. God knows what they'd have said if I'd have gone to Leeds, Bradford or worse still, Manchester. But it was time. I had to move on. I had to discover some new ghosts.

Pull into Halifax on the train and you see Beacon Hill, which looks for all the world like a freshly painted theatrical backdrop. One day it's going to fall over and there'll be two old caretaker types in smocks sitting behind it, playing Pontoon and eating digestives.

Once this bloke asked me where the train station in Halifax was. I told him it was next to the train station. He looked at me like I was being funny. I wasn't. Halifax train station *is* next to the train station. There's an old one and a new one. The old one is now part of Eureka, which is a place where kids go in the school holidays when it's raining, and the new one is, well, it's the train station. Stand in front of it and you go back in time. Suddenly you're in one of those naff costume dramas on BBC1. To the left are the India Buildings (1861), in front of you is the spire of the Square Congregational Church (1857) behind that is the Piece Hall (1779) and to the right, the grand-daddy of them all, is the Parish Church. Most of the church is medieval but parts of it are 900 years old. *Nine hundred years.* I knew it was old but that's just showing off.

It's like talking about York.

Three

7:46 Huddersfield to York

I'm standing in a queue in Huddersfield train station. People are buying tickets.

Return to Leeds.

Return to Dewsbury.

Return to the Forbidden Planet.

I made that last one up.

I never had a train set. I never wanted one. Trains didn't float my boat, if you know what I mean. They were just big noisy things that rumbled around on endless tracks in somebody else's world. Dad always had a car - the Batmobile - a runabout to get us from A to B. If we ever wanted to go to C we'd have been up the creak without a whatsit but generally, the car did the job.

The 7:46 to York came at 7:46. You can live for a hundred years and never say that, so I'll say it again. The 7:46 to York came at 7:46. It really did. I knew it was coming because the tracks began to crack and buzz and people started sizing each other up. It felt like that electric moment in a pub just before a fight kicks off. Everyone got a bit edgy. Then the train rolled into view and it's scrum-down time. Why the panic to find a seat on a train? What's that all about? Stand up. Dare to be different. People will notice. They'll think that you're an inspector working undercover. The next time you're on a train, stand up, look shifty, go up to the bloke next to you and say *Tickets please*. He will show you. I know, I've tried it.

All I see from Huddersfield to Dewsbury is a beerbelly. Not *my* beerbelly you understand. This one belonged to someone else, the someone else that decided to stand right in front of me. I think he was a tad miffed because I'd got a seat and he hadn't. Ah well, the standing will do him good. To be fair, it was a good beerbelly. As good as they get. The only problem with it was that it didn't suit the man it was attached to. He didn't have the beerface or the beerlegs, just the belly. He had a round body with sticky out arms and legs. He looked like a kid's drawing.

The beerbelly got off in Dewsbury and suddenly the sun came out. I looked out of the mucky window and saw a sign on a mill: SHODDY AND MUNGO MANUFACTURING. Shoddy and Mungo? Sounds like two over the hill clowns on the run from the Moscow State Circus. I can imagine a tearful Shoddy turning to his grease-painted mate and in a voice heavy with Smirnoff and regret, saying – *Where did all the fun go Mungo?* Besides Shoddy Manufacturing? Pull the other one.

The bloke behind me is on a mobile phone.

Ello hun, yeah love, OK babe, sure thing chick.

Hun, love, babe, chick? Is this all one woman? And he hasn't finished yet.

OK petal, yeah, right darling, see ya soon sweetheart.

The man's either a sex god or he's forgot who he's talking to. I sneak a glance at him. He looks like John Prescott. So, he's forgotten who he's talking to then.

When we arrived in Leeds everybody got off, the big city was calling. I wasn't listening and stayed on the train. I was looking for something. I was trying to find out where Leeds turns into the Vale of York, where the West becomes the North. There's the odd clue dotted about. When you cross the Wharfe the land slows down a bit and puts its feet up. There are no stone walls and the cowless fields look back at you like big blank faces, but on the whole you can't see the join. You'd go bog-eyed looking for it. It's like staring at one of those Magic Eye pictures. Everything morphs into everything else.

The Vale of York?

I never liked that. It's always the Plains to me, far better. Not the Plains of John Wayne, cattle drives and men wearing stetsons, but the Plains of history, blood and battles that happened right here on my own doorstep. Vales? Come on. Would you fight for something that widows blow their noses on?

Exactly.

Pocket Size

Old Coat, Olde Hatte

I'm sitting in the Olde Hatte wearing the Crombie. I'm drinking a pint of John Smith's and listening to two conversations.

One: *(man with beard to another man with beard)* – Let me give you some advice, always stand behind a shooter and in front of a shitter, that way you'll never get shot at or shit on.

Two: *(old lady with no beard to another old lady with small beard)* – Do y'know when the Americans went to the moon, my mother said, what've they gone to our moon for eh, why do they always have to take what's ours?

Sometimes all you have to do is listen.

The Grand Old Duke

I'm here. It's early in the morning and I'm standing on Lendal Bridge eating a perfect bacon sandwich: brown bread, no butter, black pepper, brown sauce. To my right I can see the Norwich Union building, in front of me is the Maltings pub and way over to my left, across the river, are the twin towers of the Minster tickling the sky. Ah yes, it's the Grand Old Duke himself. Say hello to York.

I wasn't going to do this.

A million and one people have been to York and written a million and one things about it. The world would tick over quite nicely thank you without me banging on about the place. That's all you need. Talk about the other Yorkshire, I tell myself, the Yorkshire that no-one knows about, the bits they don't put in the brochures. Who wants to read about the Romans and the Vikings again, about Constantine the Great and Eric Bloodaxe? Who cares that the Minster took 250 years to build or the fact that the Shambles look a little bit more shambolic every day? What's the big deal about Guy Fawkes' birthplace or Dick Turpin's grave? Who gives a monkey's about the Battle of Stamford Bridge in 1066 where Harold beat Harald only for Harald to beat Harold a few days later in a little rematch they call the Battle of Hastings?

Well, I give a monkey's, a big monkey.

York is York is York. I had to go, writing a book about Yorkshire and not writing about York would be to write a book with a big hole in it. It would be a cop out, the literary equivalent of decaffeinated coffee or alcohol-free lager. Leaving it out would be just too political, people would get miffed and go around saying - *What's up with him, what's he got against York?* The fact is I've got nothing against York. As cities go it's got everything, in fact it's got more than everything. It's got amazing buildings, a world class racecourse and good pubs, it's got a real buzz, a big coffee coloured river running through the middle of it and more history than you can shake a stick at. What more do you want? Going to York would be a day out, a trip back in time, I'd enjoy myself.

So why wasn't I going to do it then?

When I was a kid we used to go on daytrips to Scarborough, Filey and Whitby. We'd mess about on the Wharfe at Bolton Abbey and go picnicking on Shipley Glen. When we felt more adventurous we went further afield to strange, exotic places like Blackpool, Cornwall and Chester Zoo. Not once did we go to York or if we did, I can't remember. And that's the thing: I have no inner memory of York, nothing I can call my own. York as a city is an amazing place, you can't argue with that, but as an idea, a memory, it just doesn't belong to me. It's the things that you see, smell, feel, touch, hear and taste when you're first becoming aware of the world and your own little place in it that you keep with you. It's those experiences that make us who we are. York, I'm afraid, has nothing to do with me.

But hey, maybe that's a good thing.

When I read those million and one things about York I feel like I'm reading about Peru or Mexico, about the Incas and the Aztecs. As a kid York felt that far away, it was at the other end of the world, even now it's hard for me to believe that the place is a one-hour train ride from my front door.

I can forgive York for not being part of my past, water under the bridge and all that. I can forgive York for making me feel like it's in another country. No problem there. I can even forgive York for Terry's Fruit Jellies but what I can't forgive is the tangible effect the city has on me. Whenever I go to York the place robs me of something and makes me feel like a tourist in my own county, *my own county,* the bloody nerve. I go for a coffee, I feel like a tourist. I read the plaques on the old buildings, I feel like a tourist. I look at the posters advertising the floodlit cruises and the ghost walks, I feel like a tourist. It's just not on. The last time I went to York I actually held street maps under my coat so no-one could see what I was doing. I'm a grown man for God's sake and York makes me feel like a kid having a quick peek at the top shelf mags in the newsagents. It has to stop. It's embarrassing, it's ridiculous and it's unforgivable.

So what's to do? Maybe I'm missing something here and approaching this all wrong. I mean what's so bad about being a tourist anyway? York's chocabloc with them and they all seem to be having a beano. Maybe that's the way to approach it, just step back and go with the flow. Yeah, that's it. This time I'm going to York and I'm going to be objective. I'm going to be a blank canvas and let York paint itself all over me. If I have to be a tourist in the very county where I was born then so be it. If that's what it takes then bring it on. This time I'm going to be Dwayne from downtown Detroit and Tanizaki from Tokyo. I'm going to be a bloke from Berlin called Boris. I'm serious. This time I'll leave myself behind and get lost in the crowds. This time I won't be a Yorkshireman.

The first thing you see is the wall. It's big and old and makes York look like a holiday camp, a kind of medieval Butlins. Walk on it and you get a good view of the city and of the people trying to stay warm on the open top buses. You try to look around, to take it all in but there is one thing that keeps catching your eye. And, as a tourist, that's my first port of call.

Whenever I see the Minster it makes me laugh. Not a big belly shaking, wheezy, help-me-I-can't-breathe kind of laugh but a little bloody-hell-what's-that-doing-here kind of laugh. I laugh because it's hard to believe that a building like the Minster actually exists right here in Yorkshire. Fancy factories like Salt's Mill in Saltaire, ornate town halls like the one in Leeds or even over-blown train stations like the one in Huddersfield, I can live with, but the Minster, the biggest Gothic building in Britain and the largest medieval church north of the Alps, *in York?* Shouldn't it be in Salisbury or Canterbury or somewhere? I'm glad it's here. I'm relieved they haven't turned it into a car park or a shopping centre. Whenever I see it I'm taken aback. That's the thing about the Minster, it never stops surprising

The Minster does something to me. I don't know what. All I know is that I feel different when I come out than I do when I go in.

It's not a religious thing. I'm not going to start knocking on people's doors, flogging copies of *The Watchtower* or anything. It's something to do with the scale of the place, the quality of its stillness, the way the sun spangles through the stained glass windows. I like the Minster because it doesn't look smug or over pleased with itself. It should do but it doesn't. It's too old for all that palaver. It does look a bit crumbly around the edges though, like it's made out of meringue, you could almost stick your finger through some of the stone work. But, for all that, the Minster has still got it. It stands there, ancient and brooding and says LOOK AT ME. I AM AN IMPORTANT BUILDING, SHOW ME SOME RESPECT.

And you know what? I do.

I sat on a bench and looked up at the window they call the Heart of Yorkshire. They call it that because it's got hearts in it and it's in Yorkshire. I looked up at the window and thought of all the other people who had done what I was doing right now, people down through the centuries, all across the world. I thought of all the Kings and Queens, the rich people and poor people, the people with pots of money and those without one to pee in, the peasants, the princes, the priests and the paupers. They'd all looked up at the Minster, they'd *engaged* with it, made a connection. I looked up at that big old window for a while. Then I looked for a while longer. Then I got neckache and looked around to see what the rest of York was doing.

It was all there.

A busker was playing a fiddly-diddly-jiggly type tune on a violin, a bored bloke in a shiny yellow council coat was sweeping the street, an old bloke was cutting the grass around the Minster on one of those little tractor thingys, Americans in their best holiday togs walked past, they were smiling and saying – *jeez, get a loada that* - a stressed out young mother was sat on the wall, she was rolling her own cigs and shouting - *bloody sit down Shane will yer* - an Irish bloke straight out of *Father Ted* was swearing into a mobile phone - *it's all a bollox* - he said - *a complete and utter bollox* - a Japanese couple went past slurping coffee from Burger King cups, a very old lady pedalled past on a very old blue bike, a very old blue man pedalled after her, a group of German schoolkids with expensive rucksacks stood listening to their teacher, they were well behaved and pretended to look interested, a student with marmalade hair was leaning against the wall eating a Bombay Bad Boy Pot Noodle, a vicar breezed past with two full bags of dry cleaning, he grinned at me and looked well pleased with himself, maybe he was the star of a new ad campaign - *Sketchley's - For the Cleaner Cleric.*

In the Minster yard is a statue of Constantine The Great 274-337AD. You can't miss him, he's the big bloke made out of stone. He's sat down taking it easy. He's got the kind of expression on his face that you see on passport photos: a combination of being too scared to move and trying not to laugh. He's wearing a great pair of comedy lion slippers, the kind unlucky dads get on Father's Day. Good old Constantine, bit of a lad but he liked a laugh. Anyway, if he was so Great why is his sword broken? I'm not making this up, the next time you're in York have a look for yourself. Maybe he broke it in a glorious battle or a fight over a woman or maybe he broke it killing the bloke who bought him the slippers? Yeah, that's the one.

The Romans liked York and called it Eboracum, which sounds a bit like Ee-by-gum, well it does if you say it fast enough. Eboracum. Ee-by-gum. Eboracum. Ee-by-gum. Well I'm convinced.

And then it was dinner time.

I knew it was dinner time because the streets were suddenly full of men wearing suits that were too small eating baguettes that were too big. They all walked past saying things like - *Did you catch that memo this morning* - and - *I happen to know that Brian upstairs in accounting isn't happy* - Oh really, well *happen to know* this Baguette Boy, I don't care.

I popped into the King's Arms down on the waterfront on King's Snaith for a pint of dinner. The King's Arms is a little battler of a boozer, a real survivor. In the winter when it rains heavy and the river gets full of itself, the Ouse breaks its banks, seeps through the King's Arms front door and makes itself at home in the front bar. Inside there are old photographs of soldiers standing in boats helping people out of the upstairs windows and, over in the corner, a polished piece of wood on the wall records how high the flood levels have been over the years. On 17th October 1976 the Ouse came up to my knee, on 2nd April 1940 it was above my belt and on the 4th November 2000 the water level was well above my head. Blimey, maybe it was best not to dawdle. A quick swig of Sam Smith's and I was on my way.

There are 60 churches in York. That's right, *60,* and that's within the walls. I mean, how many do they need? In 15 minutes I walked past St Michael's, St Cuthbert's, St Olave's, St Martin-cum-Gregory's, St John the Evangelist's, St Tom's, St Dick's and St Harry's. They've got so many churches in York that the more popular ones are putting the others out of business, I walked past at least two that were up for sale. There must be churches for every occasion: churches to be christened in, churches to get married in, churches to get un-married in, churches to go to if you're thinking about getting married but not quite sure because your fiancée is always propping up the bar in the King's Arms waiting for the next flood.

It was still dinner time so I bought a sandwich from York's Yummy Chicken and ate it on Whip-Ma-Whop-Ma-Gate Street. Opposite me was a teenager sat next to his mum. You could tell it was his mum, they had the same nose. He was pointing at the street sign and talking to her.

Whip-Ma-Whop-Ma-Gate, he said, is the shortest street in England.

Really? his mum said.

He nodded.

Oh yeah, he said, I know that because it's a Trivial Pursuit question.

Really? his mum said again. She smiled that smile that mum's save for their sons when they tell them useless information. I used to get it all the time.

Mum, did you know that Geoff Boycott scored 48,426 runs for Yorkshire?

Really love, that's nice.

Yeah and did you know that Yorkshire covers more than 6,000 square miles?

Really?

Later on, when you got wise to it and knew she wasn't listening, you could say anything you like.

Mum, did you know that I'm never going to school again because it's rubbish and boring and I'm going to be a astronaut or a rock star anyway so I might as well stay in bed all day, eating Mars Bars and cream buns and chocolate biscuits and drinking Tizer and playing my records really loud and watching Tiswas and The Six Million Dollar Man?

Really love, that's nice.

I skulked around going nowhere and ended up outside the Job Centre. Next to the Job Centre is the Jorvik Café, Corals the Bookmakers and the Stonebow Snooker Club. I suppose that if you've got nothing to do all day then it's good to know that you've at least got somewhere to do it. There was a group of blokes leaning against the wall. They were smoking and staring at nothing and even though it wasn't cold they all wore woolly hats and big coats. One, a thin bloke with a fat face, had a Crombie on that looked like mine. He smiled at me and I smiled back. He made me feel like I was a member of a secret club. He asked me what time I was signing on.

Half two, I said.

I didn't want to let him down.

These blokes looked like they needed someone to speak to, to have a chat and pass the time with. They looked like they wanted a hand, a leg-up, a spot of TLC.

Where's the dry cleaning cleric now? That's what I want to know.

I shambled my way to The Shambles and saw a lot of people pushing mountain bikes. Hang on a minute, mountains, *in York?* Have I missed something here? Have they shipped some in from Tibet and plonked them at the end of Colliergate? Can you see the peak of K2 from Bootham Bar or the snow-capped tip of Everest from Micklegate? Or are people just being silly?

People are just being silly.

The Shambles, like the area around the Minster, is where York is at its most Yorkish. Up on the modern precinct, with its Thomas Cooks, Nationwides, HSBCs, Pizza Huts and Marks and Spencers, you could be anywhere but just one look at The Shambles and you know you're in York.

The Shambles started life as a meat market where the town's butchers used to live and work. It might look cute and tourist-friendly now but at one time The Shambles was oozing in guts and fresh offal, sheep-heads and old hooves, rusty bone saws and blood-soaked cleavers. The timber-framed houses and meat-hooks are still there but these days The Shambles is nothing like the battlefield it used to be. The Shambles has disowned its roots, had a serious makeover and turned itself into a new place. It's lost something and I think that's a shame. I'd have loved to have seen The Shambles in its heyday, it would have been a great place to throw a bucket of yesterday's tripe out of an upstairs window.

I made my way up The Shambles to King's Square where I sat and listened to a bloke with a big beard and long hair playing cheesy love songs on a battered upright piano. He was using a Utterly Butterly margarine tub as a money box and looked like a Viking version of Liberace. *I Just Called to Say I Love You* and *Wonderful Tonight* I could handle but when he played the opening bars of *Lady in Red* that was it for me. I was out of there.

I parked myself in the Last Drop Inn on Colliergate with a pint of Yorkshire Terrier and tried to figure York out. I still felt like a stranger here, an outsider. Being a tourist was hard work. I'd tried not to be a Yorkshireman and I'd failed. I just couldn't put York out of my mind and pretend that it was all fresh and new. It's not that simple. I think my relationship with York is like York's relationship to the rest of Yorkshire. York is North Yorkshire. I'm West Yorkshire. York is Harrogate, Helmsley, Malton and Thirsk. I'm Halifax, Bradford, Leeds and Huddersfield. The differences are everywhere. They're geographical, cultural and historical. The Industrial Revolution pretty much by-passed York. It got as far as north Leeds and called it a day. It didn't do that with me. Oh no. The Industrial Revolution rolled up its sleeves, put on its big muddy boots and trampled all over the old woollen towns that make up my neck of the woods. Then, because it was having such a good time, it marched into South Yorkshire and did the same. That kind of history stamps its mark on you. I've got far more in common with the traditional coal and steel towns of Sheffield, Rotherham, Doncaster and Barnsley, than I have with York. In fact, if I'm being honest, *really* honest, I've probably got more in common with Manchester than I have with York. So there, what do you say to that?

Really love, that's nice.

Under a Big Sky

Let's call him Toothless Bob.

There he is. He's standing at the foot of Ribblehead Viaduct and he's painting. He looks arty and interesting, like he's walked out of 1930s Paris: beret, paint-splattered pants and goatee. He is wearing a T-shirt with PAIN IS WEAKNESS LEAVING THE BODY written across it. He looks good until he opens his mouth.

He hasn't got a tooth in his head.

His mouth is just a big wet hole in his face, an open wound. Bob's smoking a roll-up and giving the canvas a good coat of looking at. The painting is top notch. It's alive with movement, depth and energy. Bob knows his way round an easel and pallet alright, no doubt about it. He should paint himself some teeth. The only problem with his picture is that it's a painting of the sea.

I don't get it.

Maybe I was wrong. I look at the picture again: waves, seagulls, little boat bobbing about, yep, that's the sea alright. I have to say something.

Looking good, I say.

He grins a gummy grin.

Can I ask you why you're painting the sea, I say, when you're looking at Whernside?

Toothless Bob looks me up and down, takes a good drag on his roll-up and lets it out slowly.

Because sometimes in life, he says, you have to invent your own oceans.

Then he flicks his roll-up away and goes back to his painting. Inventing your own oceans. I like that, I don't know what it means, but I like it. Good man Bob, shame about the teeth.

It was the kind of day when great things happen. Elvis was born on a day like this. So was Groucho Marx, Frank Sinatra and John Wayne. It was on a day like this that they invented the wheel, found out the world was round and discovered penicillin. Fred met Ginger on a day like this, Stan met Ollie and Lennon met McCartney. The sun has got his hat on.

Hip, hip, hip, hurray.

It was that kind of day.

I'm standing at the bottom of Whernside and I'm looking up. Big hills are only good from a distance. When you're on them all you see are other hills. Whernside was looking good. Considering it's been around a while the old boy scrubs up well. I've come to here because Whernside gets overlooked. Pen-y-gent and Ingleborough get all the press, they're the ones people rave about. It's that distinctive flat-topped duo that you see on the postcards, calenders and tea-towels. Whernside gets pushed into the wings. It's the highest point in Yorkshire but it doesn't bang on about it. Maybe it should. It's the bit-part player, the straight-man. Whernside is the Ernie Wise of the Three Peaks.

Today though, I'm going to give Whernside centre stage. It's got the spotlight, the best dressing room and the pick of the dancing girls. But before you get to the top you have to sit through the warm up act. Ladies and Gentlemen, please welcome, the Ribblehead Viaduct.

It's big innit.

Stand in front of it and tell me it isn't. Ribblehead Viaduct is so big it makes the 18-carriage freight trains that cross it look like toys. The best thing about it is that it doesn't know when to stop. It's having a ball and just keeps on going. Every archway just cartwheels into the next one. It's a big stone smile 44o yards long. Ribblehead Viaduct is the happiest Victorian building in the world.

The 24 arches that make up the viaduct were handmade and God knows what the men were like who built it. There were no Health and Safety inspectors back then, no JCBs and jackhammers, no hardhat and boots. Pain wasn't weakness leaving the body to these men. To them pain was a way of life. A lot of them didn't make it. They'd give all they had and couldn't give any more. The weather, the disease, the broken bones and the backbreaking grind of it was all too much. Nobody knows exactly how many men died building the viaduct but they ran out of space in the local graveyard at Chapel-le-Dale. A lot of men didn't get that far and were buried in rough graves on the moor. Nameless men who came from nowhere and lived a grim life full of gruel and graft. The men who built Ribblehead were a special breed, carved from the same stone as the viaduct itself.

Things are getting seriously rural. I know that because the flies are getting bigger. I'm walking on springy mud and being stared at by springy sheep with little devil faces. I know they hate me. As I pass Blea Moor signal box some clouds float over and stamp the moor with shadow. Suddenly the world is the colour of a pool table in a dodgy pub. The sky is getting bigger and the path in front of me is getting smaller. Behind me Ingleborough is playing tricks. The farther away I go from it, the bigger it becomes. How does that one work? Then it dawns on me. It's the landscape. That's how it works.

Landscapes are full of magic. I know this bloke called Rob who went to Peru to check out the lost city of Machu Piccu. Lost cities always have cool names like Machu Piccu, they're never called Heckmondwyke, Cleckheaton or Pontefract.

Rob was on one of the mountains in the Andes when a heavy fog came out of nowhere. Ah well, he thought, I'm in no rush, I'll sit down for a quiet ponder and see it out. He sat there a while, then he sat there a while longer and then he started to think deep thoughts.

How deep? I asked him.

Very deep, he said.

I was interested.

Were these thoughts about the Incas and how they worshipped the Sun? I said.

No, Rob said back to me.

Were these deep thoughts about how the Incas used to call silver, The Tears of the Moon?

Nope.

I kept pressing.

Were these deep thoughts about how the Incas used to cover the roofs of their temples with gold?

Rob looked at me.

I wasn't thinking about the bloody Incas, he said.

I was getting somewhere.

So what *were* you thinking about then? I asked him.

He pulled on his earlobe.

I was thinking about my old bird in Kippax, the one who gave me the elbow.

Rob pulled on his earlobe again.

I've never really got over it, he said.

That's landscapes for you. The Andes might be the Andes but broken hearts are bigger than mountains.

I'm standing on the stone bridge over Little Dale Beck and the top of Whernside looks further away now than it did when I started. It's the way the hill is made and how the path zig-zags its way up to the peak. From this angle it looks embarrassed with itself, like it's told a joke and nobody's laughed. On my left is Force Gill Waterfall doing its best to giggle. Underneath my boots are copper coloured puddles and above me is the sun. It's still wearing a big hat. Things were getting hot and sticky. The Crombie wasn't doing me any favours.

I made the turn at Knoutberry Hill and walked onto the ridge, the back of the whale. The big old hill was warming to me now and starting to open up. Dentdale unfolded itself way down on my right. It looked a million miles away. Everything went quiet. Whernside was getting ready for me. It was setting out the placemats and polishing the best china. Below me Greensett Tarn looked like the outline of some obscure South American country. Swallows were dive-bombing me. They wanted to keep the place to themselves and who can blame them. I followed an arrow straight stone wall all the way to the summit.

I'd done it.

Here I was, under a big sky, standing on the roof of Yorkshire. I was looking down on everything - York Minster, Bolton Abbey, Leeds

Town Hall, the M62 - they were all down there. I couldn't see them. I didn't need to. I could feel them. They were inside me, swimming around in my head. I had to do something. I wanted to celebrate like footballers do when they score. I should have worked out a routine. I wanted to run and dive on the grass. I wanted my mates to give me bear-hugs and slap me on the back. I squeezed my eyes shut tight and made a mental snapshot. I raised my arms up and grabbed the sky. I wanted to hold on to this moment and never let it go.

Ever.

The landscape was doing its stuff.

I started having deep thoughts.

I thought about Uncle Jim and his dogs. I thought about a horse called Double Vodka and a man called Truth, about Rampant Rabbits, chicken bhunas and Samuel Webster, about bungalow legs, Rocky Bigfield and the Ursa Major man. I thought about cotes and shelters and home. I thought about a lot of things, about this and that, everything and nothing.

Oh yeah, the landscape was doing its stuff alright.

I'm in the Station Hotel at the foot of Whernside. I'm sat opposite the Loo with a View and listening to a tinny radio playing old songs in the background. If this was a cheesy made-for-TV film, then Louis Armstrong would come on singing *What a Wonderful World*, but it's not and he didn't. I've taken the Crombie off and I'm having a breather. I'm drinking Copper Dragon bitter and eating a Giant Yorkshire. I go through the Crombie pockets and find a bus ticket, a return train ticket to Barnsley, a screwed up bookies' slip, a couple of scribbly beermats and an old crisp packet. That just about covers it. It's the little things that tell us who we are.

I finished my Yorkshire, put on the Crombie and went to catch the train. I didn't have to wait long. The 19:17 to Leeds came bang on time. With a bit of luck and a fair wind I'll be in the Olde Hatte for last orders.

Hip, hip, hip, hurray.

I told you it was that kind of day.